The English Room

THE ENGLISH ROOM

Derry Moore and Michael Pick

Weidenfeld & Nicolson

London

Frontispiece
The Galleried Hall, Madresfield Court

Designed by Trevor Vincent

George Weidenfeld & Nicolson Limited
91 Clapham High Street, London SW4

Filmset by Keyspools Limited, Golborne, Lancs
Colour separations by Newsele Litho Limited
Printed in Italy by Printers Srl, Trento
Bound by L.E.G.O., Vicenza

Contents

CONTENTS

Foreword
by Anne, Countess of Rosse

BROUGHT UP in two beautiful houses enriched by rare collections, I was well schooled to observe and appreciate the nuances inherent in the English room. All of my own five houses have been totally different in style, date and size. I have been happy in all, but have never wanted to intrude upon or change the aura I loved. In each case I have tried to belong to the house rather than the house to me; to let it remain itself but to enhance it a little in its own way. I lean on a mélange of things I treasure and have never boasted of 'good taste'. Yet detail matters: flowers and a warm fire are as important as beautiful furniture. A room *'trop bien arrangée'* is fussy and unrestful. Only our beautiful Paine ballroom at Wormersley has had the helping hand of a decorator who, proudly, was none other than John Fowler to whom the English room owes so much.

What differentiates English rooms from those of other nations is that they are primarily rooms for living in, not only for looking at. They reflect immediately at all levels the personalities and whims of the people themselves in whose houses they are, their individual tastes (or no taste at all!) and their way of life. The ideal English room breathes welcome, ease and effortless imagination. We often mix superb period furniture, *objets d'art*, valuable paintings and tapestry with 'things we love'. Great-uncle Elmo's elephant-leg umbrella-stand looks quite happy next to an exquisite piece of early *cloisonné*. Family photographs do not necessarily ruin the balance of a Louis xv table and the little things made by one's children sit cheerfully on the chimney-piece.

When I inherited 18 Stafford Terrace, the charming Victorian house which inspired the founding of the Victorian Society, Cecil Beaton threw up his hands in horror. 'Can't she make just one room normal?' he shouted. 'But dear Anne has always loved clutter.' A certain amount of clutter is essential. Remember that it is very often raining in England so that life is frequently lived indoors. English rooms must radiate a calm and reticence forming a sympathetic background for occupation or work lasting for hours on end. Books should abound, needlework and always and ever a well-equipped writing table with a wastepaper basket to boot. Comfortable chairs, cushions and footstools will invite intimate tête-à-têtes and parties. In the dining room we strive to create an atmosphere that will be sympathetic and inspiring to lively conversation and laughter, whether for four or for twenty, with deliciously simple English food and flattering candlelight.

This most fascinating survey of the English room spreads its wings over the widest variety of styles, tastes and characters of the English people and their way of life. It transports us from the grandest and most ambitious of palaces and castles to architectural masterpieces of all dates and forms and even to humble terraced town houses and cottage rooms. Superbly illustrated by Derry Moore with his sensitive eye for shapes and colours, each example of the English room is here given generous appreciation and understanding by Michael Pick, so that the individuality and immense variety of the rooms is apparent and welcoming to all in this enchanting book.

Introduction

Tʜɪs is neither a history of the English house nor of English decoration, both of which have been more fully described by others. It is a survey of that most elusive concept now so often misrepresented and misunderstood by decorators and their clients: the 'English Room'. No slur is cast on the rooms of Scotland, Wales or Ireland. To consider all the variations and nuances of style contained in those countries would require a far larger book and would deviate from our central theme of investigating the essential English qualities captured in the photographs. Inevitably, certain aspects of the history of architectural and decorative styles are discussed as various rooms are scrutinized and dissected to uncover different qualities, all reflecting national characteristics. These are indeed varied and often highly eccentric. A mid-nineteenth-century American view of the English by Ralph Waldo Emerson in *English Traits* (1856) is still applicable to the style of our most English-looking rooms: 'Every one of the islanders is an island himself, safe, tranquil, incommunicable.' In this book Emerson describes the very stuff of which England was – and still is – made: an assertive, inventive and rich nation, one slow to change, but remarkably receptive to outside ideas and influences, which are assessed and then utilized to the advantage of its people.

Since Emerson wrote his appraisal we can see the development of another trend in English life, that of a distaste for sudden change and upheaval. Many of the rooms pictured here reveal a blending of all these characteristics in an interpretation of old styles. This disinclination to be 'up to date' was already manifest in 1934 when Evelyn Waugh wrote *A Handful of Dust*. The owner of a Victorian mansion in a medieval style reacted in horror to his wife's modernization of one room, and his lady friend 'stirred the mouldings of fleurs-de-lis that littered the floor, fragments of tarnished gilding and dusty stencil-work. "You know, Brenda's been a wonderful friend to me. I wouldn't say anything against her . . . but ever since I came here I've been wondering whether she really understands this beautiful place and all it means to you."' Every room in this book has an individual quality which is the personal response of an Englishman to his surroundings; each reflects both the country's heritage and the capacity of its people to assimilate outside influences in a unique way.

For nearly two centuries there has been an acknowledged export of an English style to America. The world of the late nineteenth century, described by Henry James and Edith Wharton, was one which first experienced the lucrative beginnings of an export trade in English antiques to America, whilst England imported heiresses to bolster the fortunes of its noble families. This two-way traffic slowly spread an aura of exclusive 'chic' to the very concept of a room decorated in the English manner, so much so that even in France the possession of English antiques, or of rooms pretending to be 'English', is now a status symbol. Once French rooms were universally more 'chic' than English in the illustrated journals devoted to decoration; now French antique furniture is no longer the most sought

Opposite The Music Room, Alnwick Castle

9

after, and the enormous rise in the value of English antique furniture over the past five years is the conclusive measure of this. Record prices have been paid, usually by non-English buyers. Never has the 'English room' been more in demand, and the desired look is no longer simply that of the seventeenth or eighteenth centuries, but also of the late nineteenth century and more lavish Edwardian periods.

No-one doubts the existence of an English style of decoration, but the definition of such a style varies with every attempt at explanation. Why does a room look specifically English rather than French, Italian, German or American? Furniture alone does not give the look of an English room, and nor is the use of chintz a yardstick for measuring 'Englishness', as many contemporary decorators would seem to believe. There must be certain qualities apart from the furniture which contribute to an English look, and these include the choice of fabrics, carpets, decorative objects and paintings, as well as fittings. Whatever the architectural style of a room the effect can be made 'English'. In the history of post-Renaissance English architecture only the Perpendicular and 'Tudor' styles can claim to be truly English in origin, for all other styles derive ultimately from foreign sources; the English look must therefore emerge not from specific architectural references but by mastering a diverse range of styles and foreign influences. The ability to create this look is an inborn trait which may be developed but not acquired, and an examination of the illustrations in this book will reveal what is an instinctive decorative skill. Most of the rooms are not the work of professional decorators creating a setting entirely from their own resources; they are rooms that have evolved to fulfil the needs of the owners.

In his 1955 series of BBC Reith lectures, 'The Englishness of English Art', Professor Sir Nikolaus Pevsner gave the personal view of an academic observer. His German background gave him a clearer and more detached perspective as he pointed to 'those features in our national character which inspire in our art its essential Englishness'. His lectures affirmed the English genius for the assimilation of apparently contradictory beliefs and ideas as well as of decorative styles from abroad, all of which are fused into something essentially English. With an incisive Germanic erudition he separated influences and new inventions, ranging from 'the immense international influence of Palladianism, the Picturesque garden, Robert Adam and Wedgwood, to the equally all-embracing influence of English iron construction, to the great art of landscape painting in the early nineteenth century and its influence in France, and to William Morris, the so-called Domestic Revival of the late Victorian decades, and the idea of a garden city'. He arrived at the conclusion that, 'What English character gained of tolerance and fair play, she lost of that fanaticism or at least that intensity which alone can bring forth the very greatest in art.'

In the creation of English rooms, an often transient but no less demanding branch of the arts, we must often disagree with Pevsner, for examples such as the work of Adam and Chippendale at Nostell Priory (pages 46–9) are manifestations of English genius ranking as the very greatest. Pevsner himself recognized that most subtle of English achievements, the use of light as a decorative medium. He admired the early-nineteenth-century house of Sir John Soane in Lincoln's Inn, London, in which the Monk's Parlour relied on sources of light that were concealed from the visitor's eyes by the architectural structure of the room.

The subtlety of English light is perhaps the greatest dictator of English tastes: from the high clear skies of late spring and early autumn, to the soft twilight of damp winter days and the golden aura of a fine summer, our eyes are accustomed to changing shades and depths of colour. The Elizabethans were the first to embrace this wonderfully varied English quality, and the size of the windows at Wollaton Hall in Nottinghamshire, Longleat House in Wiltshire, or Hardwick Hall in Derbyshire, reflect not merely the settled state of the country, becoming peaceful and progressive, nor the wealth of the owner, but also the feeling of being a civilized human being living in ordered surroundings. The rooms at Hardwick are not particularly remarkable for their size (the halls of earlier castles and houses were just as large), it is the construction which is of importance. The foremost reason is summed up by the old jingle, 'Hardwick Hall, More glass than wall.' Built by the formidable Bess of Hardwick between 1591 and 1597 the house was an affirmation of her position in society, and her initials were carved in the commanding heights of the decorative stone parapets. She could afford the expensive glass, and she could also afford to rely on the unfiltered light of the Derbyshire Peak District as the principal decorative element in her house. No need to fortify windows or fill the interior with particularly sumptuous or expensive decoration, her powerful status is seen rather in the revolutionary form of the architecture. Apart from tapestries, decorative plaster and woodwork, the furniture was mainly simple and sturdy with great patches of colour coming from various wall-hangings. The forms of the windows and fireplaces already show an awareness of the architecture of both France and, primarily, developments in Renaissance Italy, but although such influence is undeniably present it is still true to say that Hardwick represents a truly English style – and of the 375 workmen recorded as working on the house not even one had a discernibly foreign name. When Britain was at the zenith of her imperial and industrial might in the nineteenth century this style was revived for its apparently true English roots. It gave a spurious ambiance of antiquity to acquired fortunes, and seemed to assert that Victorian men were equally as cultured and worldly as the dashing adventurers of the Elizabethan era.

When revived by architects such as Anthony Salvin the style became known as 'Jacobethan', and although the huge windows were reintroduced, as for example at Alnwick Castle (pages 8 and 72–3), they were not leaded but formed of sheets of plate glass. The strong light they permitted was now subtly filtered by blinds and heavy drapes in deference to more decorative interiors. The extreme reaction aroused by the Modern Movement and such houses as The Homewood (pages 116–17) often centred on the immense quantity of glass used as walling and the consequently very strong light in small rooms. The modern 'picture window' may be a novelty of the years after the First World War as far as using one sheet of glass is concerned, but windows using leaded glass covered just as large an area when Sir Francis Bacon was writing his *Essay on Building* at the turn of the sixteenth century. He was actually advancing the complaints of the twentieth-century house dweller: 'you should have sometimes faire Houses, so full of Glasse, that one cannot tell, where to become to be out of the sunne or cold'; even then Englishmen were wary of new developments in architecture.

For centuries the English lived for the most part in gloomy and uncomfortable surroundings, cooking and heating by means of open fireplaces and only putting a premium on comfort by the end of the sixteenth century. The large number of houses that survive from the seventeenth century show how firmly established the search for comfort had become by then. The Romans had introduced a form of central heating to England but this was ignored for almost fifteen hundred years, and even Robert Adam in the eighteenth century relied on open fireplaces to provide heat, for his study of Roman decoration and architecture was more aesthetic than scientific. He did attempt a form of central heating in at least three buildings, including Kedleston Hall (pages 38–9) and Newby Hall (pages 44–5.) From the time of the Normans in the eleventh century, the fireplace came to be moved from an open place in the middle of a large hall to a convenient construction made of masonry against a wall, connecting to a flue and chimney. Four centuries later they were simple constructions such as that in an Oxfordshire country house illustrated on pages 16–17. The slow development of the fireplace forms a barometer of taste in reaching the sophistication of a carved marble chimney-piece in the eighteenth century, as seen in many of the interiors illustrated in this book. Even today there is something peculiarly English about an open fireplace. Clean and efficient stoves were established components of continental rooms by the eighteenth century, particularly in northern Europe. They remained rare in England, where a general taste for central heating only became well established in the 1960s.

A fireplace is by its very nature a dominating fixture in any room and has often held the portrait of the house-owner above it, so that one feels at the very heart of the house. The Library at Hatfield House (opposite) has a Venetian mosaic of Robert Cecil sunk into the wall above the fireplace that forms part of the decoration of the chimney-piece. The size of the fireplace dictates not merely the decoration of a wall but also the scale of its decoration and often that of the whole room. The positioning of the furniture will also stem from the various properties of the fireplace and the chimney decoration, determining size, composition and style. Given that other walls will hold doors and windows it can be appreciated how limiting a fireplace can be on the decoration of a room, particularly in winter when the fire is needed. It is fascinating that such a form of heating with all its attendant draughts and discomforts should have survived in England for nine hundred years. Even a Modern Movement house such as The Homewood retains a fireplace and in the smooth monolith of the grey-black Levanto marble wall a flickering bank of flames mocks the expanse of plate-glass windows and the hot-air ducts beneath (page 117).

An appreciation of the subtleties of English light, the craving for a visible warming flame in the hearth; these are dominant factors in the decoration of English rooms and few decorators or their clients now fully appreciate either. They can learn from Robert Adam's Marble Hall at Kedleston Hall (pages 38–9), where firelight will bring the cold alabaster to life, or from Mrs Syrie Maugham's rooms at Upper Grosvenor Street, dispelling all hint of the foggy atmosphere of 1930s London with Venetian colours and a fireplace glowing in the Bathroom (pages 110–13). The love of warmth and light and a longing for their incorporation into an English setting are part and parcel of the decoration of English rooms. Ultimately a room's success or failure can be judged on the quality of colours, materials and objects, and the manner in which all these are handled. This is a subjective process, but, as Mrs Nancy Lancaster has so rightly reminded us, the decoration of a room should be blended in as delicious a manner as a well-mixed salad.

Opposite The Library, Hatfield House

Few decorative schemes can match the apparently effortless brilliance of the Library at Nostell Priory (page 46), an English triumph of blended tastes if ever there was one. It seems unnecessary to have to understand the motives of either a decorator or an owner (or both), one's own initial reaction should settle the matter of whether it appeals or not. But an understanding of the planning behind a room may turn dislike into a degree of appreciation, even if dislike is rarely overcome. In this book the photographer's skill has often changed near-geese into swans, because he has known the elements to emphasize – some rooms, like some people, are not photogenic.

When Erasmus visited Britain in the 1490s he wrote with distaste: 'The floors are commonly clay, strewed with rushes, so renewed that the substratum may be unmolested for twenty years, with an ancient collection of beer, grease, fragments, bones, spittle and everything that is nasty.' Because of the difficulty of keeping any floor particularly clean until the early nineteenth century, the objective was to conduct life on surfaces well away from the floor. Furniture had high legs and was built for sitting up, and the decoration of rooms was scaled around such comparatively high furniture; for even in the houses of the very rich the floor could never be kept as clean as it is today. By the 1980s, however, the pertinent observer Quentin Crisp was noting a very different social phenomenon: 'It is always possible for anyone to judge the financial status of his host by the distance of the table tops and chair seats from the floor. The higher the income bracket, the lower the furniture. In Miss Deterding's house all horizontal surfaces were well below the knee' (*How to Become a Virgin*, 1981). His remarks reflect a complete revolution in decoration and domestic arrangements.

Much of our decoration today is undoubtedly a form of nostalgia for the past, and in particular for the apparent comfort of the Edwardian era. The look and atmosphere of the English Edwardian country house, with overtones of royal visits, is a style of decoration attempted so often as to elicit a groan and a yawn. It is as though the spirit of one of Lady Londonderry's housemaids has insinuated itself into the hearts of some of the most crusty of Englishmen and most sensible of Englishwomen, all longing to be part of Edwardian England: 'It was after one of these Royal visits [by King Edward VII] that [the then] Lady Londonderry had dressed early and, happening to go down into the drawing room before dinner discovered one of the house-maids with a duster in her hand sitting on all the chairs in the room by turns. With great intuition she immediately guessed the reason for this curious behaviour. "That is the chair His Majesty sat in," she said, pointing: "now have a good sit in it."' (The Marchioness of Londonderry, *Retrospect*, 1938).

There are many stilted re-creations of would-be Edwardian rooms. Few have bothered to sort out the more appealing elements and adapt them to our own day. Successful interpretations are often almost subconscious and result in such delightful interiors as those of Lady Rupert Nevill at Horsted Place, Sussex (page 56), or the Duchess of Beaufort (pages 128–9). This form of nostalgia is fostered by some decorators and appears to have succeeded the desire for an eighteenth-century room. (That look was popular for the first sixty years of this century, but the finest English antique furniture of that date has become so expensive that only the serious or status-seeking collector will buy it.) But it also has its roots in both the Shell Guides of the 1930s and then the social upheaval of the Second World War and after, when such publications as *The Saturday Book* were creating a nostalgic image of a fast-changing and vanishing Britain in a series of beautifully produced and illustrated articles and photo-essays that continued through the 1950s and 1960s. The nostalgia extended to surveys of English arts and crafts and a glimpse of idyllic country life, all cats and singing kettles. Even if the editors of *The Saturday Book* admitted as early as 1946 that cottages of the type illustrated in this book were already virtually extinct (pages 30–1), the pressures of wartime life had sharpened ideas and feelings in crisis and clarified nostalgic thoughts only half-felt in peacetime. 'We have a tendency to mourn the disappearance of places we have never seen, or of which we know nothing,' wrote James Pope-Hennessey in *History Under Fire* (1941).

Through the whole of English decorative history run very rich veins of individuality and eccentricity, veins we can trace through the writings of so-called 'social observers'. The Victorian diarist Augustus Hare is an invaluable source of lively gossip and anecdotes. He was related to many of the oldest families of England, however distantly, and made the best possible use of his contacts. He was almost a professional guest, travelling around Europe and Great Britain recording anecdotes and descriptions of domestic surroundings in town and country, published in six volumes between 1896 and 1900 in *The Story of My Life*. The Frenchman Louis Simond was a similarly fascinating and highly critical observer of the English, visiting Britain to investigate agricultural and industrial progress just after the Napoleonic wars, when England presented a rich variety of widely differing lifestyles, housing and industries to his sharp eyes. His impressions were published as *Voyages en Angleterre pendant les années 1810 et 1811*, in 1817. Both men described the eccentricities of their hosts with a certain astonished admiration. I, for one, feel great sympathy for Lady Harriet Wentworth, visited in January 1881 by Augustus Hare. He found her in the precincts of what he termed her 'great Italian Palace' at Stainsborough, Yorkshire, 'Wentworth Castle': 'I do so hate the thraldom of civilization,' she told him, and he went on, 'Her stately rooms have no charm for her, and though they are so immense, she declares that she cannot breathe in them, and she lives entirely, and has all her meals in the conservatory with a damp, warm, marshy climate from which she does not scruple to emerge into the bitter winds of the Yorkshire Wolds (for the conservatory does not join the house) with nothing extra on.' And indeed, what is an English room without at least some hint of an English garden and the countryside to breathe life into it?

An Oxfordshire Country House

THE COUNTRYSIDE is full of houses such as this, houses which have evolved naturally and are still enjoyed as comfortable and beautiful homes. Given the ancient architectural features of this sixteenth-century country house it would be difficult not to create an interesting atmosphere, although not easy to acquire from scratch the furnishings we see here.

The powerful arch of the Dining Room fireplace (opposite) dominates the scene and is the centre of attraction when lit – a room within a room. Apart from the fire-irons and implements the area is enlivened by the marble bust placed in the brick recess: in the light of the flames it creates an uncanny effect. Unusually, the brick surround leading to the chimney has been whitened and this is a clever way of diminishing the otherwise overpowering effect of the great size of the fireplace. The trestle table is seventeenth century. There is an Italian feeling of warmth and colour which is generally absent from English houses of this period and is in part attributable to the three busts of varying origin on display, and to the paintings in their gilt frames. The needlework of the chairbacks and the carpet is of course in characteristic English taste, as is the blue and white Chinese garden seat. The incongruous juxtaposition of all these objects is part of the character of this house.

The extraordinary triangular window in the Study (above) is thankfully left uncurtained and emphasized by a stark modern sculpture. It is the main source of light for a sensual painting, completely dominating one wall in spite of the heavy beams and door. Through the open door the eye is led on to another large canvas, and the warmth of fleshy bodies lends the room a vitality and interest quite remote from the hard white walls and tough beams. Whether the paintings are correct in scale, date or subject matter for the house is of total irrelevance. The owners have utilized their possessions and surroundings originally and to the best advantage, and have created a fascinating atmosphere.

Loseley House
The Surrey House of James More-Molyneux Esq.

THE Great Hall forms the heart of this Elizabethan house built in 1562 by Sir William More, at a carefully recorded cost of £1,640 19s 7d. He was adviser to Queen Elizabeth I, but the house is not comparable in scale or design to such a building as Hatfield House (pages 20–3). There is no grandeur, but a sense of domesticity which has acquired a mellow charm. The Hall reflects warmth and hospitality and still holds the appeal it undoubtedly had on the three occasions when Queen Elizabeth visited it. It was probably also the scene for the anxious calculations of the enormous cost of entertaining the Queen and her retinue.

A large square-bayed oriel window lights the far end of the room, and other windows high above the panelling keep the room bright. Although a large fireplace (not visible in the picture) is the main feature, the room is completely dominated by the canvas depicting Sir More Molyneux and his family. They have gazed down on the scene since 1739 and the house was then already antiquated, not just old-fashioned. But the room is full of charm

and pleasant things and it is not surprising to find it still loved and used. A comfortable mixture of sofas, antique chairs of various periods and mellow panelling is a background for the paintings. That of Sir More and his family is so enormous that the room's size is immediately diminished to less overpowering proportions. The colours give warmth to the uncurtained windows and stonework, and this is also reflected by the panelling; that on the wall below Sir More's portrait is thought to have come from Henry VIII's Nonsuch Palace, built at Ewell in Surrey for Catherine Parr. It was demolished in the late seventeenth century, and the decorated panels to either side of the chimney-piece are also thought to have come from there. The room therefore contains elements reminding us of episodes in English history and portraits by Kneller and Lely (among others) conjure up the spirits of generations of the family. The room is as comfortable now as it has even been since first built more than 400 years ago, gaining in charm as the room mellows with age.

Sissinghurst Castle
The Kent House of the Hon. Nigel Nicolson Esq.

WHEN Vita Sackville-West and her husband Sir Harold Nicolson bought Sissinghurst Castle in Kent in 1930 there were only four ruined buildings standing, fragments of the original Elizabethan mansion. The two new owners created the beautiful gardens, the focal point of the setting.

The arrangement of the buildings allowed for each of the four members of the family to live quite separately, giving the privacy essential to both authors. Miss Sackville-West's Sitting Room, situated on the first floor of the tower where she could 'see without being seen', is an intensely personal and private room: no family chatter echoes here. Plain wooden bookshelves, simple curtains, buff papered walls: in these surroundings Vita wrote her many books, her weekly gardening articles for the *Observer*, and the vast number of letters she sent regularly – even daily – to her friends, husband and sons. The strong Tudor arch and octagonal table with great lion paws dominate the scene, although the low divan is clearly of the inter-war years and reflects the 'studio' look of much contemporary decoration. Over the well-used brick fireplace are stepped shelves more typical of southern Germany or Austria, but which did occur in England; the turquoise ornaments are part of Vita's large collection of coloured glass, and provide a brilliant splash of colour. Paintings are positioned without any formal arrangement, or concern for scale. Books line the walls and little alcove, and follow the octagonal shape of the turret: they include her own and her husband's works, source books for her biographies, as well as books on travel, literature and, of course, gardening. It is a practical living room, without pretension or self-consciousness. The couch and carpet are shabby and worn, they are there for comfort not effect and possess a charm that only age can create.

Hatfield House
The Hertfordshire House of the Marquess of Salisbury

HATFIELD HOUSE has been the seat of the Salisbury branch of the Cecil family since the present house was built by Robert Cecil between 1607 and 1611. It was his reward from James I, for whom Cecil had secured the succession to the English throne from the dying Queen Elizabeth I. Cecil became High Treasurer and principal adviser to the King, and set about rebuilding Hatfield to make it a worthy reflection of his status. Apart from the substitution of plate glass for the leaded lights and the screening in of the colonnade on the façade, the look of the house has remained relatively unaltered for centuries.

Only the Great Hall (page 22) survived the construction of the new building. Cecil supervised the details of planning and construction with the architect Robert Lyminge to advise him, and it is a curious building revealing something of the new owner's aspirations. The 'E' shape is said to commemorate Elizabeth I. Cecil was clearly gifted in many ways and the building reflects the taste of an Elizabethan Renaissance man, interested in the arts as well as affairs of state. There are strange anachronisms in the design which incorporates a Long and North Gallery and a Great Hall of enormous size, filled with Italianate Renaissance detail carved into the English oak panels and beams. Cecil must have conceived these rooms as a reflection of his new status as first Earl of Salisbury, and no doubt envisaged meetings of great state importance occurring there; but he died in 1612, having spent over £38,000 on the house and only eight nights there.

The Grand Staircase (opposite) is one of the less overpowering pieces of design in the house, and is historically important as one of the earliest free-standing English wooden examples to survive – that at Knole is earlier still, but less sophisticated. The carved newel posts become alternately figures or heraldic beasts above the arcaded balustrade. Rather crude strapwork decorates the plaster under the stairs. On the walls are some of the paintings admired by Samuel Pepys on a visit in 1662. The house and gardens (designed by Salisbury in collaboration with John Tradescant) did not excite the admiration of everyone. As a contemporary verse pithily put it:

Here lies, thrown for worms to eat
Little bossive Robin that was so great
Not Robin Goodfellow, nor Robin Hood
But Robin the encloser of Hatfield Wood.

It might seem impossible for a house such as Hatfield to disappear given the history of the family and site, but a period of neglect under the sixth Earl (1713–80) saw Hatfield fall into decay.

According to Augustus Hare: 'He died a death as horrible as his life. His is the phantom coach which arrives and drives up the stair-case and disappears. Lord Salisbury heard it the other night when he was in his dressing room, and dressed again, thinking it was visitors, and went down, but it was no-one.' Luckily the sixth Earl's son James had a political career and no doubt kept up the house as a firm symbol of his family's ancestry.

In 1835 the same Earl's widow was incinerated in the West Wing, having suffered an accident with candles in her bedroom. 'It would have been impossible to identify her ashes for burial but for a ruby which the present Lady Salisbury wears in a ring,' wrote Augustus Hare on 14 December 1872. Danger to guests was also present in other forms: 'In the drawing room, over the chimney-piece is a huge statue of James I in bronze. It is not fixed, but supported by its own weight. A ball was once given in that room. In the midst of the dancing someone observed that the bronze statue was slowly nodding its head, and gave the alarm. The stampede was frightful. All the guests fled down the long gallery.'

Still the house survived and came to be of great importance again as the third Marquess involved himself in politics: he was three times Prime Minister to Queen Victoria and was the first to combine this office with that of Foreign Minister. It is from this period that the Library dates. The third Marquess was interested in scientific experiments, and had a room equipped with apparatus; he introduced electricity to the house, and even had a rudimentary telephone system installed in the Library (pages 13 and 23). This room has a look of sober politics, the books, leather upholstery and dark woodwork are all evocative of the House of Lords. The room is also a splendidly restful evocation of the flamboyant Renaissance style of the house. We can see how the carved pilasters are separated by the various colours of the book spines. Below are simple neo-Classical pilasters, while above on the gallery are neo-Renaissance details, along with a modern construction for the cast-iron balustrade. The detailing is a slimmer, more delicate version of that found on the Grand Staircase. The furniture is a mixture of contemporary cabinets with Regency and Sheraton chairs and settees, and the worn old leather gives a warmth to the room which is lacking in the white and gilt ceiling. This is English neo-Renaissance, as much as the Italian decoration at Alnwick (page 72–3), and the well-worn upholstery exudes a comfort that is lacking in Alnwick's more formal setting. It is nevertheless a distinguished room, redolent of tobacco smoke and the discussion of politics, in a Hatfield tradition nearly 400 years old.

Hatfield House

Opposite The Great Hall *Above* The Library

Nymans
The Sussex House of Anne, Countess of Rosse

THE SPIRIT of the famous gardens begun by Ludwig Messel in the 1890s has entered this house, so that both are fused into a tranquil expression of English country-house living. This is not his house. His undistinguished late-nineteenth-century villa had replaced an eighteenth-century farmhouse which stood on still earlier foundations, but the present house was built by Lady Rosse's parents, Colonel Leonard and Mrs Maud Messel, in the 1920s. One whole wing, including the Hall and Library, was destroyed by fire in 1947 and remains as just a shell. The remaining wing, the home of the present Countess of Rosse, has the comfortable look of a Cotswolds manor house built of stone in the late-sixteenth or early-seventeenth-century style. The effect was undoubtedly more Oxbridge College than Surrey Stockbroker when new; and that this taste for late English Gothic should still be manifest in the 1920s says little for the contemporary architecture and much for the strength of English traditions. Time has mellowed the stone and the ruined wing gives a spurious additional quality of age, particularly

as creeping plants encircle the empty oriel windows and finger the sharp outlines with a green embrace. Rhododendrons, camellias and magnolias are famous ingredients of the gardens laid out with the aid of such experts as Gertrude Jekyll; and inside flowers everywhere give a sense of warmth and colour to the robust architecture. In vases, pots, or as patterns on fabrics they insinuate the garden's spirit into the whole house.

In the Countess's Oriel Bedroom (opposite) is a comfortable mixture of modern and antique English furniture, mainly of the late eighteenth century, softening the uncompromising lines of the window, chimney-piece and recesses. The draped dressing-table is a particularly charming and feminine touch amongst such austerity, but chintz curtains, a yellow-covered easy chair, the brocade bed-cover formed from an eighteenth-century Italian clerical fabric, and a tray-table all lend warmth to the room, whilst the elegant cheval glass gives light and sparkle to a corner. Pleasing touches are added by items of family memorabilia, like the walking

Nymans

Opposite Mrs Messel's Bedroom *Above* The Dining Room

stick hung over the fireplace with *moiré* ribbon: it is a Linley heirloom from the eighteenth century.

The seventeenth-century furnishings of Mrs Messel's Bedroom (opposite) create the romantic surroundings that are so much a part of inter-war decoration, as in Hollywood's evocation of Manderley in Daphne du Maurier's *Rebecca*. Part of the charm lies in understatement: no use of dominant colour, but soft hydrangeas, the marquetry of the William and Mary chest-on-stand, the tapestry on the wall and in the fire screen, all reflect the garden, as does the great oak bed with posts as strong as young trees and a counterpane as soft and inviting as an English bowling green. The soft pinks and reds of the carpets glow against the mellow woods and light walls, welcoming the visitor to a restful night's sleep.

Comfort and hospitality are captured in the Library (page 25), which houses an outstanding collection of books on flowers. The muted colours of covers and chintz curtains are enlivened by the books' spines, and flowers are arranged to suggest the informal life of the country. Lady Rosse worked the needlepoint cushions. Although the room has old English furniture, it is distinctly twentieth century in appearance, the past being a pleasant background.

Bygone ages are more strongly suggested in the Dining Room (above), once the maids' sewing room, where a mixture of furniture of different periods subtly suggests the natural development of a long-established English house. A simple seventeenth-century oak dresser base blends with an early-nineteenth-century looking-glass with a well-decorated giltwood frame. The blue and white porcelain, some Delftware, some eighteenth-century English and some oriental, is arranged with an eye for proportion and effect, and graceful Regency chairs cluster around a simple early table. This fusion of styles is as English as the gardens which are the dominant presence throughout the house.

Weston Hall
The Northamptonshire House of Sir Sacheverell Sitwell

WHEN Sacheverell Sitwell went to live in this seventeenth-century house in early 1928 he found a timeless atmosphere conducive to reflection and writing. The faded grey stone of the exterior was surrounded by lush gardens and fine old trees, amongst which the later Gothick decorations to the façades gain a comfortable softness of outline. Weston Hall was left to Sir George Sitwell by his aunt Harriet, Lady Hanmer, but was intended for his son Sacheverell. Sir George was typically difficult about handing over the house outright, and teased with his ideas for it, saying 'I don't intend to do much here; just a sheet of water and a line of statues'. The house was to be administered by trustees. Its simplicity was appreciated by Sir Sacheverell, who always used a bedroom as his study: 'Too fine a view from a window would also be an impediment to writing. There should not be, and in any case there

are not, too many flowers. The room, it is true, is much too small, but I am used to it . . . having spent some four to five hours every day, during seven to eight months of every year, in this room, writing. From quarter or half-past nine to half-past twelve, and again from five o'clock to seven. Every weekday, on Christmas Day, Easter, Whitsun, all public holidays, and *always on Sunday* which works out at about seven years on end here "in solitary" in this room, working and looking out of the window' (*For Want of the Golden City*, 1973).

Ordered calm is steeped throughout the rooms and the objects in them. In the Justice Room (above) is nothing to disturb the eye or alarm the senses. Against a soft background of pale lilac walls and white woodwork is ranged an unusual pair of black lacquer cabinets on stands: they hint at trade with the Orient and the British

love for 'japanned' or lacquered furniture and objects. Together with the elaborate frames of the mirrors they form the major components in a scheme linking various types and styles of furniture. Birds, stuffed and under a glass dome, or painted and set in lacquered frames, remind one of exotic and local climes. Bronzes and mirrors give movement and light to the eighteenth- and early-nineteenth-century English furniture and a decorative floral border applied to the walls links objects and colours. The room has an unusual mixture of objects; and the red glass in the door is typically unexpected. The furnishings are all unlikely pieces to accompany one another, yet combine to give elegance to a peaceful interior.

The Library (above) has a vibrant quality which is in contrast to the soothing furnishings, which include an early-eighteenth-century walnut armchair and a sensible library drum-table laden with books. The sparkle comes from the delicate portrait of Dame Edith Sitwell by Pavel Tchelitchew, painted in 1929. The colours of the painting are reflected in the room; but in spite of the rather intrusive turquoise lamps and the book spines, it is the portrait that holds a magnetic power. One of six paintings of Dame Edith by Tchelitchew, it lay behind a cupboard in her Paris flat throughout the war years until retrieved by her secretary Elizabeth Salter in 1959. Dame Edith gave the startling opinion that her relationship with Tchelitchew was 'exactly like the relationship between Vittoria Colonna and Michelangelo'. It was certainly one of considerable emotional torment, and to the artist she had the 'green-gold hair and most beautiful nose any woman ever had'. The painting has a strength and strange beauty quite in sympathy with the atmosphere and decoration of this ancient house.

Two Traditional English Cottages

NOSTALGIA is an English passion. There has been no era in our history when we have not looked back to another age for either inspiration or comforting glimpses of what we imagine our own age should be. These two cottage interiors charm by their evocation of a cosy, bygone era. They are comfortable homes that have so far escaped the tide of gentrification. Can they really still exist? In many such cottages forests of paper with artless designs in peculiar combinations cover the walls. On broad swathes of nylon, flowers become geometric shapes and are pinned down by the polystyrene comfort of a three-piece suite angled at the household gods of TV and electric or gas 'log' fire. These rooms represent an England as traditional as Anne Hathaway's Cottage, with simple, centuries-old decoration for comfort. The former inhabitants of the 'gentrified' cottage are now in neat modern bungalows.

Already in 1946 *The Saturday Book* was accurately recording immediate post-war changes with contrasting photographs of a Somerset cottage and Queen Anne's bedroom at Warwick Castle, captioned 'This, and the parlour ... are socially and respectively rare and common. Yet the cottage hearth has qualities, domestic and aesthetic, as rare as the castle chimney piece, and still rarer in point of survival.'

Both the cottages illustrated here rely on the open coal fire for warmth and decoration. Britain, as Aneurin Bevan once pointed out, is secure in being an island built on coal. Take away the fireplaces here and there is no heart left to either house. These rooms are unself-conscious arrays of trivial furniture and decoration. The Gloucestershire cottage (above) has a fireplace blacked in a manner which even the proudest Northern housewife, as so

vividly described in Richard Hoggart's *Uses of Literacy* (1957), would gloat over. This is a fully working survivor of the millions of ranges once found throughout Britain. They heated the living room, provided cooking facilities with hot-plates and oven, even heated water through a boiler built in behind the grate. Other countries had enclosed stoves, but D. H. Lawrence's mining heroes could bath in their tin tubs in front of a hot coal fire. The range dominates the whole room, although the framed photograph of the soldier has such a magnetic poignancy in its association of simple English cottage life with service in the British Empire overseas that the eye is drawn automatically to it. China, glasses and a 'Royal Memento' are all essential elements of the cosy atmosphere.

This also applies to the Dorset cottage (above) with its equally welcoming fire set in a brick grate framed by a wooden mantelpiece. The whole decoration of the room is built up around this glowing hearth. A mirror sparkles above, Staffordshire pottery dogs and knick-knacks are peculiarly English in their odd shapes. Niches to either side contain books and useful pieces of furniture – including a TV set. The snug Victorian chair might have sat there for decades, for the room is timeless and so planned for comfort that there is no reason for change.

In neither room is there anything strident or flashy, nor is there anything to indicate a change from Ralph Waldo Emerson's view of 1856 when he wrote: 'The stability of England is the security of the world.' These rooms afford a tranquil welcome and pretend to be nothing other than cosy.

Chatsworth
The Derbyshire Seat of the Dukes of Devonshire

UNLIKE MANY palatial houses Chatsworth is more welcoming than most and this is partly due to the quirky floor-plan and adaptation of spaces to their present use; it is also due to the way the house visibly displays changes in taste and ownership. The present Duke's ancestress Bess of Hardwick would have approved of the decision by William Cavendish, fourth Earl of Devonshire, to demolish her house of the 1550s and build his own in 1686. This house has a distinctive English baroque style both inside and out, and although the four elevations of the exterior were not planned at the same time and were designed by different hands, they have achieved some coherence. However, successive generations have spent much time and money trying to impose a sensible floor-plan on the muddle created inside. The Entrance Hall was thus once a kitchen; and the staircase, which leads up to the inconveniently positioned State Rooms on the second floor, has been replaced three times in an effort to generate the right effect – the present version was built in 1912. The architecture of Chatsworth appealed to Louis Simond in 1811, but not the interior. He found the tapestries in bad taste, and the pictures even worse: 'It is truly inconceivable how someone with the cultured taste of the Duchess of Devonshire could put up with such decoration.'

Much has changed since then. The Lower Library (opposite), by Crace, is a pleasant light room furnished with pieces in maplewood, particularly popular in the 1840s. It is full of clutter and useful desks and writing surfaces. Unobtrusive bookcases are banded by Italianate painted decoration.

The walls of the Yellow Drawing Room (above) are hung with a silk fabric from India. A finely carved chimney-piece of white statuary marble has heads of putti which pout into the room, and a gilt overmantel glitters above. A portrait by Tintoretto looks down on to a comfortable country-house jumble of objects, and light reflects off the sparkling Waterford lustres on the chimney-piece.

Honington Hall
The Warwickshire House of Sir John Wiggin Bart

E IGHTEENTH-CENTURY plasterwork reached sublime heights of craftsmanship and here we see fine detailing, as good as at Ditchley or anywhere. Hall, Saloon and Boudoir are decorated with plasterwork that approaches an English rococo style, all to be found in a red brick stone-dressed Carolingian house of modest design. Even more remarkable is the fact that it seems to be of entirely English craftsmanship with no Italians involved: it was carried out in the mid-eighteenth century for the owner Joseph Townsend by either Charles Stanley or Thomas Roberts under the guidance of a local craftsman, William Jones. It is remarkable that they could have produced such wonderful work.

The floor of the Hall is now smothered by a beautiful carpet, a distraction from the lightness of the scheme which relies on the black and white decoration of the floor for a definite contrast. This is also true of the club fender, which obscures the fine proportions of the chimney-piece. There is a charming intimacy about this room that embraces so much fine decoration.

Ditchley Park
An Oxfordshire House Decorated by William Kent

I N THIS COUNTRY HOUSE of the early 1720s James Gibbs created an austere Palladian exterior, thankfully enlivened with the elaborate interiors devised by William Kent and Henry Flitcroft. English plasterwork reached perfection during this period in a manner unlike that of previous centuries. The English Baroque was given a freshness by such Italian master plasterers as Artari and Bagutti. Gibbs employed both, and one of them may have produced the design and work for the Saloon (above) with its warm yellow curtains and walls of sienna marble colouring, admirable in contrast to the stark white of ceiling and wall decoration. In this English variation of an Italian style we can see a unifying element in the detailing of the dado and ceiling decoration, contrived to unite a bold scheme that embraces an asymmetrically placed chimney-piece, elaborate plaster relief, framing surrounds, putti, mirror and pilasters. They are all linked one to another in a manner seen off and on for the next 200 years as successive generations played with this unifying technique. It can

be seen again in Sir Mervyn Macartney's work of 1890 at 167 Queen's Gate (pages 96–7).

Here the sophisticated plasterwork should be seen with the views of the grounds through the large windows, so that artifice and Nature are linked in a peculiarly English manner. It is also to be set in the context of the adjoining Great Hall and famous White Drawing Room with its Kent door and picture surrounds. When Mrs Nancy Lancaster owned the house (as Mrs Ronald Tree) the White Drawing Room was given an imaginative touch by the use of fine antique furniture: a large coromandel lacquer screen, massive gilt and marble-topped tables, sofas and a Lely portrait of Charles II gave it a distinguished air. In the spirit of her business partner John Fowler, she did not repaint the rooms, but had them stripped to reveal the glowing original colours beneath. This tangerine-like pigment was probably mixed into the plaster in the Italian manner to give the solid depth of colour we still see, but her furnishings have mainly gone.

Houghton Hall
The Norfolk House of the Marquess of Cholmondeley

HOUGHTON is a delicious triumph of architectural genius, both inside and out. This is rare. Colen Campbell's designs for the house appeared in his huge compendium of elevations and plans, *Vitruvius Britannicus*, in 1725, but Campbell did not complete the building. Instead Sir Robert Walpole, Prime Minister 1721–42, employed Thomas Ripley to execute Campbell's designs, with certain alterations and modifications. He created a building admired since completion, not least by Catherine the Great, who bought most of Walpole's fine collection of Old Masters from his profligate grandson. The collaboration of William Kent, Vasari and Michael Rysbrack on various rooms has left us a vision of the antique which surpasses that of the English Renaissance. Nancy Lancaster said that Houghton taught her 'the most': Kent's apple-green velvet-hung bed 'brings to mind a waterfall'.

William Kent was responsible for the decoration of the State Rooms. Above the fireplace in the Stone Hall (opposite) is a deep relief by Rysbrack in the neo-Classical manner, as are the reliefs on the walls and over the door. Although the influence of Palladio lies heavily on Campbell, Kent's interpretation of his ideas is handled with ease and ingenuity, and he evokes more the spirit of the Venetian or Roman Renaissance, rather than the later, more academic copy-book 'antique' of Robert Adam. For what softens Kent's inventive interpretation of Italianate styles in this forty-foot cube is a judicious mixture of fine furniture and textiles. The giltwood arm and side chairs have curvaceous legs terminating in strong claws and the show-wood is decorated with shell motifs. Covered with the original green velvet, this suite glows against the rich colours of the carpet covering the stone floor.

The Marble Parlour (above) is just as strongly Italianate in feeling. Kent's handling of the columns, pilasters and plasterwork is as masterful as Rysbrack's carving of 'The Sacrifice of Bacchus' over the fireplace. If the carrara marble seems frigid, this mood is soon dispelled by the twelve giltwood chairs blazing with Genoese velvet, and by the Venetian references in their decoration.

Kedleston Hall
The Derbyshire House of the Viscount Scarsdale

AT KEDLESTON, DERBYSHIRE, Robert Adam was presented by Sir Nathaniel Curzon with an unsatisfactory building begun by James Paine. It seems that as a result Adam must have gained a reputation for correcting or modifying the mistakes of others, for he was also called in to complete what Paine had begun at Nostell Priory (pages 46–9). As at Syon House (pages 40–3) and elsewhere, Adam used Joseph Rose Jr to execute his plasterwork. He began work on the house in 1760, finishing the Marble Hall in 1763.

Adam undoubtedly knew of William Kent's Marble Hall at Holkham, Norfolk, completed by 1759, but at Kedleston the scale is lighter and more intimate, and the detail more refined. The ceiling is left light and airy with a graceful design of Roman motifs, while at Holkham the heavy ceiling is only made possible because the floor is sunk into the basement storey to give the room an impressive height. Far from being a basilica like Kent's Hall, the Hall at Kedleston is based on the idea of a Roman atrium and the columns are firmly set into the floor and do not seek to overpower the visitor by means of great plinths. The alabaster is local. The room is entered under a form of screen created by free-standing columns, but at the other end of the room Paine's original building forced Adam to set the columns flanking the door against the wall, thus reducing the effect of all the columns appearing to support the roof, and detracting from his probable original intention.

To either side of the room are disposed benches and fine marble chimney-pieces surmounted by painted roundels of classical scenes, with a surround of gilt plasterwork figures in relief. The steel fire-grates are said to be by Adam, and the firelight must have created a wonderful effect in the evening of a cold day, sparkling off the reflective cold surfaces of columns and floor. Dr Johnson mentioned the house in his *Diary*: 'The large room with the pillars would do for the Judges to sit in at Assizes . . . the pillars are very large and massy, they take up too much room, they were better away.' As so often when discussing aesthetic matters, he was wrong.

Syon House
The Middlesex House of the Duke and Duchess of Northumberland

THERE is so much work by Robert Adam for us to see, and even more by his imitators, that we tend to take it too much for granted. Some of his finest achievements are arguably those in which he was amending the work of others or reconstructing interiors within an existing framework; and Syon is just such a case. Adam had finished his work at Alnwick (page 72) for the former Sir Hugh Smithson, created the first Duke of Northumberland, and had high hopes of being given a free hand at Syon. But the Duke had other ideas and Adam was not allowed to rebuild the elevations of the house, so that the curious Tudor facades with their large inserted sash windows give no hint of the interior decoration and are more picturesque than beautiful. Nevertheless Adam looked back with some satisfaction on his work there: 'I endeavoured to render it a noble and elegant habitation,' he wrote, 'not unworthy of a proprietor who possessed not only wealth to execute a great design, but skill to judge of its merit.' Whereas at nearby Osterley Park Adam was able to proclaim his bold interior remodelling with a brilliantly conceived neo-Classical portico, at Syon in 1762 he had to use the Entrance Hall (pages 42–3) and not a portico to heighten aesthetic anticipation for the progression of splendours inside the house.

He achieved this by creating his own idea of a 'Roman room' using the area taken up by the refectory in the original Tudor convent. The Hall is on a lower level than the other rooms, and was devoid of all colour save for the black and white flags of the floor and a bronze copy of the 'Dying Gaul' which stands at the end of the room leading by means of a few steps under Doric columns to the Ante-Room. In Adam's own words: 'The inequality of the levels has been managed in such a manner as to increase and add to the movement, so that an apparent defect has been converted into a real beauty.' The Hall is top-lit by small windows beneath the cornice, in turn given elaborate surrounds. The plasterwork of the ceiling is one of Adam's boldest and heaviest designs. Doric columns rise from the floor to half-way up the wall and a rich entablature is echoed in the deeply coffered ceiling of the apse or half-domed alcove framing a copy of the Apollo Belvedere. This room is one of Adam's most underestimated achievements in which every disadvantage of location and scale was brilliantly brushed aside. The walls have now been given colour, so that the Ante-Room (opposite) is no longer the extreme contrast it once was.

Here we see the twelve *antico-verde* columns dredged from the Tiber and brought from Rome by the first Duke in 1765, according to an old story. Adam has created the richest possible setting for these beautiful columns, in which only the form of the doors and chimney-piece serve as reminders that this is all in England. In fact wartime damage revealed them to be scagliola, and the story of their dredging was therefore probably that of an Italian dealer selling them to a gullible client. For all his research into Roman architecture Adam only incorporated a form of central heating into a few buildings (including Newby Hall, pages 44–5), and this was not one of them. He studied in Italy with Clérisseau, admired and examined the buildings of the early Renaissance and even rediscovered the colouring of Roman buildings. All this is apparent in the Ante-Room, where the proportions, compositions and colours provide perfect background material for the columns. Here is the 'picturesque antique', Adam's main preoccupation, as his drawings of the ruins of Spalato and his aquaintance with Piranesi reveal.

In the Ante-Room the fine plasterwork smothering walls and ceiling in intricate pattern is all the work of the English master-craftsman Joseph Rose Jr. Gilt anthemions blaze against the blue painted entablature. Gilt statues stand aloft crowning the columns given Ionic bases and capitals by Adam. The scagliola floor is a richly coloured counterpart to the design of the ceiling, an idea carried out with even greater intricacy in the Dining Room next door. Lest there be any doubt about the Roman inspiration, panels of gilt plaster trophies glow on the walls. Yet this room was used by servants waiting 'out of livery'!

As an expression of English style, Syon is no more typical than any of the other grand houses built as an exercise in flaunting the owner's power and forming a lavish display of his 'taste'. It is typical in its idiosyncrasy and in its reflection of a boldness of vision on the part of both owner and architect, allied to consummate craftsmanship and a great capacity for adaptation.

Syon House

The Entrance Hall

Newby Hall
The Yorkshire House of R.E.J. Compton Esq.

THE SCULPTURE gallery at Newby Hall, Yorkshire, is one of Robert Adam's more unusual and interesting exercises in re-creating a room in the Roman style, built around a domed rotunda. The designs are dated 1772 and 1776, and the gallery reveals him to be a master technician in the handling of a complex variety of apsidal and recessed wall constructions. His patron was one William Weddell, a rich connoisseur who liked to enjoy his collection of fine works of art in the distant wilds of Yorkshire, a landscape far removed from that of the Rome he visited in 1765. His death in a cold water bath 'occurred with tragic suddenness on April 30, 1792, at the age of 68 years'.

Weddell was planning to compile a catalogue of his collection when he died so suddenly, but left no notes. We know that the great bath was originally installed in a Roman *thermae*. It is a remarkable piece of hollowed-out white and purple *pavonazetto* marble, holding 214 gallons of water. The Barberini 'Venus' is also known about. It was found by an Englishman in the cellar of the Barberini Palace and sold to Weddell, who made a down-payment and then agreed to pay an annuity until his death (the amounts involved are not known). The Frenchman Louis Simond writing in 1810–11 found the gallery stupendous and the marbles true antiques, not just the fakes so often made for rich men on a Grand Tour and passed off as rare objects, such as, for example, the scagliola columns at Syon (page 40).

There is no English reticence in the background to the marble delights. The original oil lamps stand on their carved wall brackets. The effect can be little different to that achieved in Roman times and Adam even installed a version of under-floor heating, the vents clearly visible beneath some of the statues. Some of the bases are antique marble ones, and some were designed by Adam himself. He would also have liked a marble floor, but was thwarted in this by his patron, who decided on an oak floor. Since money was clearly no object, this single detraction from the total 'Roman' effect must be regretted.

Nostell Priory
The Yorkshire House of Lord St Oswald

JAMES PAINE was employed by Sir Rowland Winn, fourth Baronet, as the original architect of Nostell Priory in 1733, but it was left to Robert Adam to embellish his work. Paine was almost as prolific a designer as Adam, and the Victoria and Albert Museum, London, contains two fat volumes of his detailed designs for decoration; but his work has solid worthiness that lacks dash. Nor were his buildings as practical to live in as they were attractive on paper, so that in 1765 the fifth Baronet asked Adam to rectify the design and remodel, much as Adam was asked to follow Paine at Kedleston (pages 38–9) and to make sense of the old buildings of Osterley and Syon (pages 40–3). But his work at Nostell was scarcely appreciated until our day, and even now it is the craftsmanship of Chippendale that arouses our greatest interest.

When Augustus Hare visited the house in January 1881 he noted in his diary: 'We went to see Nostell, a very grand but little known house of the Winns', full of splendid things, glorious tapestries, china, Chippendale furniture, but most remarkable of all, a doll's house of the last century. . . .' There is no mention of Adam, let alone Paine, and it is an interesting reflection on late-nineteenth-century taste that Chippendale should be mentioned.

The finest room in the house is in fact a collaboration of both Chippendale and Adam, for the Library (opposite) is as English a room as one might expect to find. Adam employed Joseph Rose Jr to execute the fine plasterwork and he was assisted by Thomas Perritt in creating the light ceiling that is such an excellent foil for the solid colours of the woods used below. For all their delicacy the decoration of entablature and ceiling is no more sugary in colouring than that used by Josiah Wedgwood in the decoration of porcelain. The design of the carved and pedimented bookcases is a manifestation of the restraint found in much of the finest English cabinet-making and an echo of Adam's own researches into Roman styles and motifs. The leather spines of the books give an unexpected dimension to the room, creating a form of rhythm along the wall and giving it subtle depth. The Roman forms of the

Nostell Priory

Above The State Bedroom *Opposite* The Dining Room

chairs, evident in such details as their lyre-backs, and the imperial scale and decoration of Chippendale's desk give a solid nobility to the whole scheme, one that is as durable as the presence of the painting of the room and its instigator suggests.

The Dining Room (opposite) shows evidence of Paine's work in the more florid design of chimney-piece, overmantel decoration and ceiling plasterwork. The Adam details in the form of great swirls of strictly delineated Roman pattern to either side of the chimney-piece cannot be said to add to Paine's scheme, but the overall effect is very comfortable with a long set of capacious side chairs upholstered in figured velvet ranged around the gleaming mahogany table.

In the chintz-hung State Bedroom (above), the *chinoiserie* decoration and furniture set against hand-painted wallpaper were all provided by Chippendale. This room is completely English in the way it is handled, but one is nevertheless surprised at how well all the varied elements of decoration blend together. England was famous for chintz in the mid-eighteenth century (page 57), indeed a list of processes long since vanished achieved effects at which we can now only guess, for they have perished or lost their finish. Here the windows and bed are hung with a fabric that is at odds with the *chinoiserie* decoration of the furniture and wallpaper, yet it is all pulled together by the beautiful yet grotesque looking-glass.

Downstairs is now made comfortable with a flaming yellow colour scheme in the former Breakfast Room (page 47) full of pictures, eighteenth- and early-nineteenth-century furniture and full-blown festoon curtains to cut out the Yorkshire weather. After a fire at Nostell in 1980 David Mlinaric advised on the restoration, and in this room he re-used a Paine chimney-piece (originally in an upstairs bedroom) in an overall reinterpretation of the mid-eighteenth century. The room is more in the spirit of Paine than Adam; but more than that it is an indication of how varied the interior of an English house can be, as successive owners and decorators stamp their taste into the fabric.

Royal Lodge
The Windsor House of Her Majesty Queen Elizabeth the Queen Mother

ALTHOUGH this house has only existed in its present form for little more than fifty years, it has an atmosphere of age and a strange beauty that is essentially English. Because of royal ownership the house has experienced momentous events, yet it possesses the spirit of a family house and has witnessed all the joys, griefs, anxieties and expectations that any home will contain. It also breathes the English country air of Windsor Great Park and is full of flowers and plants from the surrounding informal gardens designed by King George VI and Queen Elizabeth.

The portrait of the Prince Regent, later George IV, above the arched Gothick chimney-piece in the Saloon reminds us that this is part of the *cottage orné* built for the Prince Regent by John Nash and Sir Jeffry Wyatville, almost all of which was broken up on his death in 1830. It was a favourite retreat of his. Flanked by wings at either end, the Saloon (these pages) is now the main room in the house as reconstructed for the Duke and Duchess of York after the worst of the recession was over in 1931–2.

Around the fireplace is a conventionally comfortable arrangement of damask-covered chairs and sofas. The decoration might have been undertaken at any time since 1920 and has a timeless quality. Useful tables are crowded with objects, plants, flowers and books, and the huge size of the room is made an advantage by the arrangement of further sitting areas and the placing of desks near the windows. The light Regency decoration in the Gothick manner is a pleasant background for the chandeliers and large tapestry, which in turn provides a sense of scale for this huge room. The Italianate look of the giltwood and damask-covered chairs round the heavy table is emphasized by the height of the altar candlesticks, now converted into electric lamps. By placing such large pieces against one wall all the other smaller arrangements fall into place, and are unified by the enormous oriental carpet spread across the floor. The writing-table and desk provide useful working areas beneath the Gothick windows. For all the grandeur of the room the atmosphere remains that of a much-loved family house.

A Country *Cottage Orné* in the Gothick Manner

WHAT could be more joyous than this modern interpretation of a Gothick *cottage orné*, a form of idyllic country architecture which gained impetus at the turn of the eighteenth century. The use of the Gothick style has never ceased to form an element of delightful eccentricity in an English building, and few examples have achieved the warmth and friendliness seen here. This small house has more in common with Batty Langley's Gothick designs of 1742 than the later enthusiasm for Plantagenet England evident in the 1840s publication of Joseph Nash's *Mansions of England in the Olden Times*; but the date of the building is actually closer to Nash's time, and the white-painted Gothick hall chair (actually in the Drawing Room, above and opposite) is a near contemporary of the fine oriel window behind. Warm colours make the interior of this house glow with a welcoming embrace that is far removed from any lingering ecclesiastical feelings initially suggested by the form of the Gothick windows. The owner has filled the interior with a wealth of unusual English

porcelain and pottery which forms the main decoration, for the elegant English antique furniture is very restrained in comparison with this abundant pattern and colour, particularly effective in autumn and winter.

In the spring and summer the English garden blooms outside and the seasons are reflected as an integral part of the decoration. The Drawing Room's large Gothick window (above) is left undraped, revealing the view to advantage, and the garden fruits decorating the plates together with the china pigs on the table give a countrified Beatrix Potter look. The amusing low table is almost an Indian version of English Gothick with its hint of Islamic influence. Over the marble-topped side cabinet (opposite) is a good Regency looking-glass with a *verre eglomisé* panel unusually painted with fruit. The frame's Gothick-style cluster columns are naturally perfect for the house. The *tôle* tray and oil lamp are simple decorative touches, but the main feature of the room is without doubt the collection of Wemyss pottery.

A Country *Cottage Orné*

Opposite The Dining Room *Above* The Garden Room

In the room with the garden door (above) are mustard yellow decorations and a window seat for maximum enjoyment of the garden. The plates give green blobs of colour, and are a satisfying reminder of the kitchen; the Gothick style of the house is continued in the decoration of the cornice.

The Dining Room (opposite) has similar decoration, more obviously picked out. It is full of delightful details, such as the fine collection of Staffordshire pottery hens over the fireplace. With the mahogany sideboard of about 1800 is a set of eighteenth-century French provincial chairs, and the informal mixture of styles and periods is again peculiarly English and countrified.

Before the recent redecoration Cecil Beaton visited the house and wrote of his rain-drenched stay: 'I, however, was content to bask in the summery atmosphere of his pretty 1800 Gothic house with roses in Victorian vases, on china and on chintz. The house is like the home of an old aunt or of the girl in *Spectre de la Rose*!' Bolder designs and colours now reflect the mood of the 1980s.

Horsted Place
The Sussex House of Lady Rupert Nevill

THE CHINTZ CURTAINS and loose covers seen in this room are so much a part of English decoration that we tend to take them for granted. The word 'chintz' came into the English language as Britain expanded her interests over the globe and is first recorded in use around 1614; it derives from the Hindi word *chint*, referring to Indian calico cloth painted over with a design. What followed was a great technological achievement, for the British thought to combine the European technique of using wooden blocks to print on cloth with the Indian technique of dyeing the cotton with a process that fixed the colour. By the 1670s dye-fast cloth was being produced using several colours in one pattern. During the first half of the eighteenth century British products were considered the best, despite heavy competition from abroad. After the introduction of copper-plate stamping in the middle of the century production increased without any fall in quality, and competition was effectively eliminated. The early designs often depicted scenes with figures or architectural devices; the flowery designs we associate with chintz came into common use in the late eighteenth century, when they were firmly established as favourite patterns for all types of rooms. Chintz rather than silk-hung rooms such as that at Chatsworth were now in the height of fashion (page 33). With the introduction of roller printing after 1815 chintz rushed off the machines to fill an insatiable demand, and the British textile industry boomed as much from this as from the use of any other type of fabric.

The style of the hangings in the Drawing Room at Horsted Place are particularly appropriate in a house that was designed by Samuel Dawkes and built in 1851 by George Myers, formerly Augustus Pugin's builder. Dawkes was as interested in the Gothic revival as any of Pugin's followers and he created a great mausoleum of a house with loving care paid to all the fine details of staircase and chimney-pieces. When Lady Rupert Nevill moved into the house in the mid-1960s she whitened all the stained woodwork and set about creating an interior full of light and warmth. It is now more a reflection of the Edwardian period than of the rather oppressive and earnest Gothic revival, and the house has clearly benefited both from her sensitive treatment and from the advice of Martin Battersby and Carl Toms. (Battersby's wallpaper in the Gallery is particularly striking and was designed and printed in his own workshop.) The Drawing Room could so easily be dominated by the great chimney-piece of Caen stone, with its deeply recessed carving leading to a fairly small grate. However, Colefax & Fowler chintz and wall-coverings immediately lighten the whole appearance of the room and the gilding applied to such details as the dividing arch and the ceiling decoration give an extra lift. Adding sparkle to the collection of antique and modern furniture (most of which came from the Regency house previously inhabited by the family) is a mirror between two windows that sprinkles light over the collections of enamels and paintings.

'I had forgotten what a bright, sparkling kind of room it was, bright with an Edwardian brightness of chintz and cut-glass and shiny furniture and silk lampshades and long windows filled with the greenness of lawns outside' (*All My Sins Remembered*, 1965): the second Viscount Churchill was describing his parents' house in the Midlands, but the atmosphere in Lady Rupert's Drawing Room is the same. For this is an interior that is not dead or stilted, it is a comfortable twentieth-century room that makes no demands on its occupants other than to relax.

Highclere Castle
The Hampshire House of the Earl of Carnarvon

MANY nineteenth-century country houses were not unlike the great London railway stations from which owners and guests set out to enjoy the delights of country sports and entertainments. St Pancras Station, London, is not far removed from the style of Highclere, nor are the Houses of Parliament – and not surprisingly, since the same architects worked there. The Entrance Hall (above) is particularly chilly in its Perpendicular style and extends a forbidding welcome, not softened by the galleried Hall beyond (opposite). Sir Charles Barry reconstructed the house in 1838 for the third Earl of Carnarvon, the third scheme to be submitted to the Earl. The interiors shown here were executed later, after about 1860, by Thomas Allom and (possibly) Gilbert Scott.

There is undoubtedly a cool beauty to the house. The coloured marbles to floor and columns in the Entrance Hall are as lively as the fluting, arching and vaulting that supports the roof. The bright carpet is delightfully out of place in this setting, and is a desperate attempt to lend domesticity to the cold surroundings and conjure up a warm welcome in this expression of noble antiquity.

The galleried Hall is another impressive space in which sofas and chairs invite a repose hard to achieve in surroundings like these. Rich colours, a portrait of the present Earl in uniform, a high screen and an oriental carpet strike a human note, but the room is impossible to decorate in any really comfortable manner. It was undoubtedly perfect for pre-sporting activities, gatherings and for tea after a meet, but it has no other function. Law courts, Parliament, banks, railway stations: the architecture is redolent of all these and suitable for them. Barry himself was happiest designing such buildings as the Travellers' and Reform Clubs, and these are also suggested here. The owner and his guests no doubt felt at home in all these buildings, moving from one to the other with ease, and the style of Highclere shows the world with which they were familiar, staffed by many servants, warmed by huge fires, and full of chattering voices. Devoid of all this the great Halls seem still and empty, a reminder of past lives.

Calke Abbey
The Derbyshire House of Henry Harpur-Crewe Esq.

S O MUCH has been made of the fact that this elephantine house has slumbered undisturbed for decades in its hollow amongst the Derbyshire hills that it comes as no surprise to find it little more than a huge attic full of the most marvellous delights – all as fascinating as only someone else's debris can be. Partly early seventeenth century, the house was later remodelled from 1793 to 1811. The Harpur-Crewe family have lived here for generations, and with engaging eccentricity they have squirrelled away a hoard of unconsidered trifles. Certain bedrooms have remained untouched, and are crammed to bursting point with relics of former collections accumulated by deceased members of the family, who nearly all had an intense passion for collecting. There is also a touch of a good horror film to the whole house, a feeling heightened by the decoration of Hall and Bird Lobby; both reflect a style which Evelyn Waugh described as owing 'more to the taxidermist than the sculptor or painter' (*Officers and Gentlemen*, 1955).

In the Entrance Hall (above) a wooden letter-box awaits the correspondence of long dead members of the family or guests; forlornly neglected on the hall table, it survives the era of large house parties and a necessary habit of regular letter-writing. Hard hall chairs stand waiting for the messenger, dripping with rain from his journey. Horns stab the air in mute fury and in the small Bird Lobby (page 64) – now the Breakfast Room – a table laid ready for a meal is surrounded by the unblinking glares of slaughtered animals: no convivial company is suggested by their accusing glass eyes. There is no escape from the game hunter, nor from his trophies.

Amongst the elegant pilasters and brass-nailed doors of an adjoining (remodelled) Saloon of 1841 (opposite), Harpur-Crewe ancestors look down from above. The gorgeous velvets of the chairs are now shrouded in slip-covers and the piano is as mute as the cases of 'things'. This room was conceived in its present form by the local architect Stevens of Derby, who does not seem to have known quite what to do with the space at his disposal, so that the present furnishings are as good a solution as any and reflect the late-

Calke Abbey

Above 'Collection of Egyptian Curiosities' *Opposite* The Drawing Room
Page 64 The Breakfast Room

nineteenth-century desire for sociable arrangements and rather too much furniture.

Throughout the whole house is remarkable evidence of collecting passions that only become understandable in the context of the isolated position of the house and a lust to fill empty hours and days with constructive activity. The marvellous 'Collection of Egyptian Curiosities' (above) is surely a reminder of a happy escape on a Nile Cruise from the chill and ice of a Derbyshire winter; parts of a Georgian state bed still in the chest in which they were sent from London during the 1780s hint at further delights in store. It is for such remarkable items as these that the house has achieved fame, but there is more here than that.

The appearance of the Drawing Room (opposite) is a perfect example of mid-Victorian taste, as though a time-machine is in action. Decorated by Tatham and Bailey, the room dates from 1733 with later decoration of about 1810 and the furniture is now arranged in informal groupings to stimulate conversation. It is as it was arranged in 1868. Baggy chintz covers protect the fabric of the chairs beneath, glass domes fend dust off intricate arrangements of unusual objects, and light glints from the wide gilt frames on the paintings. The room is asleep. The heavy damask curtains allow enough light in to shine in the great pier-glasses of the 1840s. 'It was a room whose furnishings should have been completed by the sound of sweet silly voices, the crackle of a fire and the tinkle of a piano and the smell of freshly made tea. But all was still, airless and silent' (Stella Gibbons, *Bassett*, 1934).

Thirty years or so ago it was still possible to find less imposing versions of such a room surviving in the suburbs of most of our large industrial cities. The villas have gone now and the contents dispersed so that this house is, on a large scale, a reflection of that particularly comfortable taste, with no pretensions to grandeur, which once formed the backbone of most English decoration.

Thorp Perrow
The Yorkshire House of Sir John Ropner

WHAT would an English country house be without a good cloakroom? Everyone loves solid Edwardian fittings – a mahogany lavatory seat, heavy porcelain and shiny brass handles. The basin should have a good marble surround and sensible plate-glass mirror with a decent brass light-fitting above. Something like a club, but better. In this 1903 ground-floor Lavatory (above) is an added luxury in the abundant and unnecessary tiles and a good-sized bearskin in which Monsieur Hulot would surely ensnare his spurs. There are useful old sticks, boots, coats and capes – just in case. Also a wonderful collection of odd photographs: insignificant scenes presumably of enormous sentimental value to someone dead for at least thirty years. Best of all are the trophies, bagged by Sir Leonard Ropner, the father of the present owner. The Ropners were a family of shipowners and entrepreneurs, who bought this early-nineteenth-century house in 1897. Although the game was all shot in the 1920s and 1930s – in Kenya, Scotland and North America – it epitomizes the *style coloniale* that was so beloved of the Edwardians.

As the second Viscount Churchill wrote of Barleythorpe, his Uncle Hugh Lowther's house in the Midlands: 'It was an incredible house, bristling with claws and teeth, smelling of taxidermy. A rhinoceros with a huge stumpy nose and eyes like bicycle lamps glared down from the top of the stair. . . . As a child I approved of Barleythorpe, and so did the rest of the children, because everything in it *was* something. Coffee tables were not just tables, they were sawn-off legs of elephants. Inkstands were the hooves of favourite horses and even paper-knives had fur handles' (*All My Sins Remembered*, 1965). That sort of house is evoked here, and this form of decoration is no longer possible now that so few of the victims' descendants survive.

Callaly Castle
The Northumberland House of Major Simon Browne

VARIOUS BRANCHES of the Clavering family have lived in this house since it first rose on its site, and when it came to the present owner's grandfather in 1877 there were already 650 years of family history connected with Callaly, parts of which date from the fourteenth century. The present building is mainly of the late seventeenth century, but there are eighteenth- and nineteenth-century additions seen here.

The remarkable confection of the Drawing Room (above) plasterwork, fretted balustrade, pillars and chimney-piece dates from 1757. The plasterwork is of Italian craftsmanship, handled delicately and with restraint; its medallions depict a mixed group of poets and philosophers, among them Pope and Newton. Galleries in a room can give the occupants an uncanny sensation that they are being watched, and this is no exception. The brittle outlines of the *chinoiserie* design in the open fret of the balustrade are in sharp contrast to the plasterwork, and lend a feeling of light and fantasy to what is in any case an ethereal setting, given vibrance by the cut-glass chandeliers and table-lustres on walls and furniture. The tables are of good mahogany in the manner of Chippendale's Chinese-Gothick designs, with fine Italian scagliola tops.

The products of the Industrial Revolution held evident appeal for Major Alexander Henry Browne, who purchased the house in 1877. The glass-roofed and stone-walled Hall (opposite) was once an external courtyard, but was made into a museum for his large collection of objects, most of which were sold to the British Museum at the end of the century. The ironwork is all rather reminiscent of an early continental department store, although the Victorian spiral staircase was actually made by the Glaswegian ironmasters Walter Macfarlane & Co. Sheaves of unused lances fan over the stone. Long dead animals are remembered as their mounted heads stare out accusingly at humans below. In the depths lurks another surprise in the shape of a horse's head. Of marble, it was dug up at Ephesus in 1841 and reflects yet another aspect of the taste for collecting apparent in this remarkable building.

An Early-Nineteenth-Century Interior
Holland Park, London

THESE INTERIORS form a pleasing pastiche of an early-nineteenth-century English town house. Just as Linley Sambourne's house (page 82–5) reflects the refined aesthetic taste of the latter decades of the century, so this is a microcosm of English taste as it evolved up to around 1840. It belongs to an architect, an enthusiastic supporter of the Victorian Society, but is neither a sterile nor academic exercise in re-creating a period. It is a functional twentieth-century adaptation of the furnishing and decorating styles of the early nineteenth century.

The Sitting Room (page 71) is built around the white marble chimney-piece of a design often seen in England with slight variations until the 1860s. Above it is another typical sight, a single sheet of mirror glass formed into an overmantel reflecting light into the room. The gasolier embellished with cut glass decoration is exceptional and a reminder that gas-lighting has been with us for a long time – Brighton Pavilion's 'dragon' chandelier was already a gasolier in the 1820s. The furniture reflects the decoration that emerged as an English version of continental 'Empire', given impetus by the works of such designers as Thomas Hope, George Smith and George Tatham, and made by cabinet-makers catering for the new taste in decoration. The massive lion end-supports of the sofa remind us of the contemporary fashion for archaeological excavations arising from Napoleon's Egyptian campaigns, while the design of the chairs derives from French influences of the time. But this room is no slavish copy. Apart from the lamps, the room is brought into the twentieth century by the leopard-skin rug over the sofa, a touch of softness which disposes of what could be a stiffly formal setting. Well-draped windows provide light, and the room is given warmth by the appealing colour scheme dictated by the fine carpet and reflected in the decoration of the wall, cornice and ceiling rose. The exact colouring of earlier periods is irrelevant to the effect here created.

With the striped papered Drawing Room (opposite) we are on more dangerous ground, for the 'tented room' look of many Regency or Empire rooms has been so often misapplied that it now invites an immediate criticism of modish over-indulgence, and is aptly termed 'Vogue Regency'. However, this blue stripe is a fine and pretty variation – it was the cheapest Sanderson design on sale (4s 6d) when the owner decorated the room in 1960. The surfaces of the room are broken by a white picture rail and cornice and are given interesting lighting by means of two suspended lamps acting as up-lighters. Although the ceiling is architecturally 'tented' there is no more contrivance than this; 'tented' rooms hung with fabric were another result of the Napoleonic campaigns in southern Europe and were more commonly seen abroad. The Empire and Regency are here further suggested by a fine pair of bookcases topped with busts; a pleasing jumble of pictures surrounds the centrally positioned overmantel. The brightness of walls and ceiling is allowed to make maximum impact by the use of softer, duller tones for the upholstery and furniture, and, since this does not exactly copy 1820s decoration, a period is again suggested rather than austerely re-created.

In the Muniment Room (page 70) is reflection of a more European style of decoration, emerging from a preoccupation with Ancient Greece and the Roman Empire. It might just as well be the room of a cultured German of the period around 1820 to about 1840, with a warm reddish colour lending a background to the gilt anthemion border, mahogany cabinet and marble busts. If the wall-lights seem over-grand for a room of small scale, they are eye-catching additions to the array of framed objects and reveal an eccentricity in arrangement which characterizes so much English decoration.

An Early-Nineteenth-Century Interior

Above The Muniment Room *Opposite* The Sitting Room

Alnwick Castle
The Northumberland House of the Duke and Duchess of Northumberland

AMONGST THE many great architects of reconstruction during the mid-nineteenth century, the name of Anthony Salvin is not high on the list of favourites. This is possibly because of his predilection for the Jacobethan style, and his playful use of distinctive elements of the architectural details stemming from the English and Italian Renaissance. He was capable of fascinating and impressive work on a huge scale as at Thoresby Hall, Nottinghamshire, and Harlaxton Manor, Lincolnshire: the interiors of both are widely different and full of unexpected delights. Here at Alnwick for the Duke of Northumberland he was in a more serious mood as he 'restored' what was basically a twelfth-century castle, with later additions and subtractions by Adam, to a full semblance of a great medieval fortress. He was neither a James Wyatt nor a William Burges and this is no Windsor, Belvoir or Cardiff Castle, but what it lacks in style it gains in a subtle handling of a complex variety of shapes and masses. Where other castles have romantic terraces and suggest *Romeo and Juliet* rather than *Ivanhoe*, this is much more to the taste of Sir Walter Scott. It stands determinedly square and forbidding on the borders of England and Scotland. It has a keep, armoury and Guard Chamber to assert the long history of the Percy family's occupation of the place back to Norman times, with a dungeon for good measure. The Frenchman Louis Simond visited Alnwick in 1810, and commented on the stone figures carved to resemble defending soldiers then set on the battlements. His senses set on edge by this, he toured the dungeons and lower regions of the Castle in some trepidation: 'We saw a crenellated iron wheel with chains and trembled at the sight of this object of torture and on questioning our guide in a sort of fright, he then reassured us that this served to ring the dining bell.'

Above ground the setting is a great Italianate Palazzo. Beautiful as much of the furniture is, it is to the paintings that we look for a continuation of this flavour. Titian, Van Dyck, even Canaletto and Meissen porcelain are somehow not what one expects or hopes to see (Canaletto actually painted a view of Alnwick itself, which still hangs in the Music Room). This is an eclectic Ducal mixture which is certainly grand in its content and very English, for the various decorative styles and elements are made to work together – but only just.

On 4 November 1887 Augustus Hare found a sad party at Alnwick. 'The actual Duchess did not appear till dinner, when she was wheeled into the room in a chair, very sweet and attractive looking, but very fragile. [She died in 1890.] The Duke [6th] looks wiry, refined, rather bored, and some people would find him alarming. Lord and Lady Percy seem to be two of the most silent people in the world – she pretty still in spite of her ten children. . . .

The charming Duchess Eleanor showed me the rooms – the magnificent rooms, which owe their glory to her husband, Duke Algernon, who, when remonstrated with for thus changing a medieval fortress, said, "Would you wish us only to sit on benches upon a floor strewn with rushes?" He purchased the whole of the Cammuccini collection at Rome, because of his great wish to have one single picture which they would not sell separately. The magnificent decorations of the rooms are by Canina, but the most lasting attraction of the castle is the library, with the really splendid collection of books formed by Duke Algernon.'

The Library (opposite) is a pleasantly lit room of wonderful proportions. The reds of wall- and floor-coverings are a soft but lively contrast to the woodwork of the shelves and the spines of the many volumes housed there. To break the great height of the room with a gallery was no great invention, but it is handled with a delicacy of feeling for the light structure and the elegant brass of the balustrade railing. The large chimney-piece is not allowed to dominate the room. White marble is inset with panels of mustard yellow and topped by mirror-glass, so that light is reflected above the fire. The room now contains enough comfortable chairs and tables to fulfil the needs of the most energetic scholar, while also making a comfortable drawing room. Above all floats the coffered plaster ceiling with richly gilt decoration. It gives the room warmth and interest, echoing the comfortable clutter of the English country house down below.

Throughout the Music Room (page 8) we can see more clearly the Renaissance detailing and are struck particularly by the finely detailed woodwork. As at Thoresby, the doors are well constructed and heavily carved and to either side of the door runs a beautifully inlaid wooden dado. Again, a remarkably intricate plaster ceiling is highly decorated, and the delicate frieze was painted in Rome for the house; its pattern was often to be seen in Renaissance Italy. A team of Italian craftsmen was actually brought over to work at Alnwick. The damask-lined walls look rich and warm, smothered with fascinating portraits, mainly seventeenth century, the background for a varied selection of furniture, mostly eighteenth century and of historic interest. The room is full of light, for Salvin put in great plate-glass windows wherever he could so that we should not dismiss the room without taking into account the views which are a major (and here unseen) part of the decoration of all country houses. It is a room which demands people to make it work, to gather around the great carved, white marble chimney-piece and laugh. Such undeniably formal, semi-royal decoration is hard to live with today without the visitors and parties described by Augustus Hare.

Flintham Hall
The Nottinghamshire House of Myles Thoroton Hildyard Esq.

THIS is a mid-nineteenth-century evocation of the Italianate Renaissance, as rural as that of 167 Queen's Gate is urban (pages 96–7). Here the allure is in a suggestion of warm southern skies, as the vegetation of the conservatory (above) seems to spill into the whole room. The idea of a conservatory gained impetus from Thomas Paxton's designs for both the Duke of Devonshire's glasshouse at Chatsworth and the Crystal Palace for the Great Exhibition held in Hyde Park in 1851. The English are devoted to their gardens; a conservatory made it possible to enjoy plants inside the house out of season. Cheap coal for fuelling hot-water pipes made it practical and exploration overseas meant that new and interesting forms of plant-life were imported. But, even if conservatories were heated and orchids nurtured through the winter months, Victorian standards rarely ran to piping central heating through houses. In 1853 the owner of Flintham, Mr Thomas Blackborne Thoroton Hildyard, and a local architect added this conservatory to his ancestral home. With its little

fountain it makes an idyllic picture that could be of St John's Wood in the days of Alma-Tadema; both the fountain and the putto (a former gas bracket) are relics of the Great Exhibition. The windows and door form a neo-Renaissance screen of stout columns and rounded arches, but the furniture inside the Library (opposite) is a reminder that this is England of the nineteenth century. A large fire should blaze in the grate of what looks like a carved oak altarpiece but is in fact a chimney-piece; designed by a Mr McQuoid, it was manufactured by Holland & Sons and exhibited as a supreme piece of design at the Great Exhibition. It sold for £500. The design of central columns, arches and niches holding bronze statuettes is nicely echoed in the windows at the end of the room. The arrangement of the furniture (also supplied by Holland & Sons) and objects can have altered little since the room was originally planned. The same areas for reading, conversation, games or writing would have been appropriate in the mid-nineteenth century and there is no reason to change them now.

Holker Hall
The Cumbria House of Mr and Mrs Hugh Cavendish

Holker Hall is a pleasant rambling building set on the edge of the Lake District next to Morecambe Bay. The first house on the site is thought to have been built in 1604, and some eighteenth-century rebuilding is evident in the older surviving portions. In March 1871 the west wing was destroyed by fire and almost immediately rebuilt by the architects Paley & Austin of Lancaster in a style best described as neo-Elizabethan. It contains a series of beautifully proportioned rooms lit by enormous windows and given a wealth of detailed plaster and oak woodwork; the Billiard Room (opposite) is typical of the general style. The linenfold panelling of the dado and doors shows both the high quality of the craftsmanship and the pleasing nature of the architects' designs.

This is distinctively a man's room. At this time women generally retired to Drawing and Sitting Rooms, while the men had Billiard and Smoking Rooms in which to discuss business and other matters. A solid leather-covered chair, a high-backed deep-buttoned settle (above), the great legs of the table all befit the scene of such a leisurely game as billiards. The game derives from one called 'Pall Mall', a forms of bowls from which the London street got its name in the early eighteenth century, but it was not played on a large table until the nineteenth century. By 1907 an oval table was even being marketed! This one is of oak and the usual single piece of slate to form an absolutely flat surface, and was carved nearby. Like the light-fittings in the rest of the house, the lighting above it was installed in 1911. Elsewhere fittings were designed to be unobtrusive – in the Library the switches were hidden behind dummy books – but this room has a very different purpose and the light beams down upon the green baize. The early-eighteenth-century hunting scenes around the walls proclaim this room to be the preserve of the country gentleman.

Madresfield Court
The Worcestershire House of Mona, Countess of Beauchamp

THE intrepid Augustus Hare, long-suffering guest of so many house parties, was at Madresfield on 21 December 1892, 'a moated house with a lovely view of the Malvern hills, and full of precious collections of every kind – old books, old music, old miniatures, ivories, enamels etc. There is a Chapel, where Lady Mary Lygon watches over the musical part of the services, aided by a footman who sings splendidly and plays five instruments as well!'

The house that he saw had been largely rebuilt between 1863 and 1888 by the architect Philip Charles Hardwick for the fifth and sixth Earls of Beauchamp. Hardwick was responsible for several neo-Tudor buildings, mainly in London, and at Madresfield his use of English Renaissance idioms turned a moated brick house of true Elizabethan origins into this Victorian mansion. It has lost the intimate spirit of the original, evoking instead something much grander. Often visited by Evelyn Waugh, the inspiration for *Brideshead Revisited*, he wrote much of his novel *Black Mischief* here.

Augustus Hare would not have seen the Dining Room (oppo-

site), created from two existing rooms in around 1900 by the seventh Earl, Liberal Leader of the House of Lords. Rising through two stories, its scale re-creates a Dickensian spirit of 'Merrie England' and establishes an aristocratic medieval style much as Sir Jeffry Wyatville's work had done a century earlier. A good collection of oak furniture and old portraits is dominated by the massively beamed roof, all lit by huge windows of Gothick design. The contrast with Hardwick's rooms is intriguing: this is a more luxurious, less rigidly handled exercise in pseudo-medievalism.

The galleried Hall (page 2) has a timeless English appearance and houses a well-mixed collection of furniture: there is a long oak refectory table with its cargo of porcelain, lamps, flowers and objects, and a pretty early-twentieth-century sofa with French curves. In one corner a case full of books gives a splash of colour. Newel posts along the gallery are surmounted by heraldic beasts in the same way as earlier examples at Hatfield (page 20) and Knole.

The soft colours used everywhere are seen again in Hardwick's

Madresfield Court

Opposite The Drawing Room *Above* The Victorian Bedroom

panelled Drawing Room (opposite), where warm greens reflect the gardens and landscapes seen through the windows. A leather screen lends more colour to the decorative scheme. In a dark corner a boullework cabinet adds lustre and an elegant low table between the sofas reflects the light of a cut-glass chandelier. There is no corner without an interesting object and the triumph of the room is in containing such a huge array of apparently unconnected objects all in harmony with one another.

Upstairs is a Victorian Bedroom (above) calculated to induce insomnia in the nervous. An ebonized wardrobe built like a small cottage and a bed with ends fit for a grave menace the occupant with a plethora of serious carving. Oak table and chairs reflect an early phase of nineteenth-century antique collecting, when oak was prized and faked from old church materials.

The oriental lacquer and panelling of the other Bedroom (page 79) take us into the period of domestic *style Ritz*. The rose brocade, painted sky of the ceiling and rococo scrolls on the walls are typical of the new look in comfortable decoration which began to gain ground in the 1890s. The wardrobe is a trifle casual: no fitted dressing room here, but the effect of luxury is as evident as in Vita Sackville-West's description of the doctor's wife staying at Chevron in *The Edwardians* (1930): 'The dressing-table, the washstand, the writing table with its appointments, the vast four-poster on which some unseen hand had already laid out her clothes, the drawn curtains, the brightly burning fire, the muslin cushions, the couch with a chinchilla rug lying folded across it – all these things led Theresa from transport to transport. She lingered for a long time over the writing table, fingering all its details. There was a printed card, gilt-edged, which said:

POST ARRIVES 8 AM, 4 PM,
POST LEAVES 6 PM, SUNDAYS,
POST ARRIVES 8 AM, LEAVES 5 PM
LUNCHEON 1.30.   DINNER 8.30.'

18 Stafford Terrace, Kensington
The Former London House of Anne, Countess of Rosse

IT IS DUE to both Lady Rosse and her mother, Mrs Maud Messel, that this monument to one man's taste still survives; it has remained virtually unchanged since Linley Sambourne, chief political cartoonist of *Punch* and maternal grandfather of Lady Rosse, lived there from 1870 to 1910. To say that the house is typical of the period would be a mistake, for it contains a highly individual collection of furniture, objects, paintings and drawings. Many of the latter are Sambourne's own cartoons, but Walter Crane, Sir John Tenniel, Myles Birket Foster and Kate Greenaway are among those friends whose work is also represented. The building itself may be conventional, but the arrangement of the interior is not.

At the entrance a large doormat proclaims SALVE to all who pass. The downstairs rooms appear somewhat gloomy and it takes time to appreciate the subtle effects of light. There are so many objects, patterns and colours that one might give up too easily. But the house repays exploration. The influence of William Morris is certainly to be found – if only in the patterns on the original wall-coverings and textile hangings – but the decoration steers far away from Morris's entirely English concept of translating nature into a unified decorative scheme. Here the background may reflect Morris, but the furnishings of the main rooms do not. A small room on the ground floor (opposite) contains fine late-eighteenth-century English furniture, yet the bold oriental carpets and Morris-pattern curtains do not appear to clash with these Linley heirlooms.

Even as a town house, the English love of the countryside and foreign places permeates the atmosphere. In *The Lesser Arts* (Collected Works, Vol. XXII), Morris gives a description of the English landscape that is equally applicable to contemporary attitudes in decoration: 'Not much space for swelling into hugeness; . . . no great wastes overwhelming in their dreariness, no great solitudes of forests, no terrible untrodden mountain walls; all is measured, mingled, varied, gliding easily one thing into another, little rivers, little plains, . . . little hills, little mountains . . . neither prison, nor palace, but a decent home.'

18 Stafford Terrace, Kensington

Above and opposite The Drawing Room

In the first-floor Drawing Room (opposite and above) extending from one side of this terraced house to the other, we are faced with such a plethora of objects that one might be forgiven for wincing. It is quite remarkable that this particular interior has survived a complete revolution both in decorating tastes and in society; for the maintenance of such a room demands constant staff and attention, rare commodities today. The scale of the great 'boullework' clock on the wall is balanced by the two vases with chrysanthemum decoration on the commode beneath. To either side are mahogany cabinets giving a balance and variety to the wall, and marble chimney-pieces. Having achieved this balance, the wall is smothered with pictures jostling into a patchwork of light and colour. Sculpture and porcelain are added, the latter in a way that now seems to us peculiarly suggestive of the Arts and Crafts movement, running characteristically along a projecting cornice at picture rail height. The upholstered furniture is typically solid and occupies a considerable amount of space, as was usual at the time.

Comfort was as important as display, and both are united throughout the house, no more so than in the Bedroom (page 83). The elaborately moulded chimney-piece is typical of English decoration of the period 1880–1910 and is a type found in many interiors influenced by the Arts and Crafts movement. Very often a mirror panel was set into the centre of the top section, but here decoration is provided by Chinese pots and miniatures of Michelangelo's figures from the Medici tombs. In front stands a fan inscribed with artists' signatures, including those of Sir John Everett Millais, William Frith, George Watts and Alma-Tadema. Sambourne is depicted with his pipe in the photograph above the chest-of-drawers to the right, his drawing board propped against the easel in the Drawing Room. The early electric light-fittings with adjustable height mechanism over the dressing table are also worthy of note as a practical invention.

As the founder of the Victorian Society Lady Rosse most certainly appreciates the products and taste of that age.

84

Elveden Hall
The Suffolk House of the Earl of Iveagh

REMARKABLE as these pastiche 'Indian' interiors are, it is doubly surprising to find them inside an undistinguished Italianate red brick and stone country house of the late nineteenth century. The Brighton Pavilion is one thing, exotic inside and out, with the lure of the sea at hand, but Elveden is set amongst the cold Suffolk landscape, with clumps of conifers around: its only attraction originally was the shooting possibilities for the Maharajah Duleep Singh, who arrived here in 1863, and for the first Earl of Iveagh, who acquired the 5555 acres from the Maharajah's son in 1894. Since first seeing the name under a group photograph of a shoot in *'Chips': The Diaries of Sir Henry Channon* (1967), the life led at Elveden had intrigued me. Why, having given Kenwood to the nation and owning other houses, did Lord Iveagh choose to keep up this enormous house? Channon's brief comments for 8 January 1935 give no explanation, but the real reason must surely have been the shooting and the house's proximity to Sandringham: 'There was a fog on my return, and I arrived back at Elveden late, cold and hungry. Our guests were all still up but all fifty servants had gone to bed, and I could get nothing to eat. In spite of that, of all the Iveagh houses I like Elveden best. I love its calm, its luxurious Edwardian atmosphere. For a fortnight now I have slept in the King's bed, which both Edward VII and George V have used.' Quite clearly this house was not merely loved, but well cared for, having fifty servants as late as 1935. Even though largely asleep since the last war it has been preserved and the contents maintained until their sale in May 1984, For example, until their auction over 200 assorted oriental carpets were examined, cleaned and moth-proofed every year – a month's work for two men and a remarkable survival of an Edwardian feat.

Pastiche 'Indian rooms' form the true heart of Elveden. Much as he enjoyed the shooting opportunities in Suffolk, the Maharajah longed for home, and the rooms in his original house (opposite) were carefully constructed by John Norton after examples in Lahore and Delhi. Originally the ceiling was inlaid with mirror (which still remains) and bright colours were applied to parts of the decoration. Broad swoops of off-white paint have swept this away, and Edwardian chintz, eighteenth-century furniture, nineteenth-century fakes and china pots gave the rooms their colour and interest. But the atmosphere of this wing has remained that of war-time. Signs caution: 'Save Electricity', 'Not to Be Opened During Blackout'; others point the way to offices. The occupation by RAF

and USAF forces has given a permanent feeling of tension to the wing.

The Indian Hall (pages 88–9) is in the centre of the house, joining the Maharajah's original house with a replica and so creating a huge new house for the Iveaghs. If Duleep Singh's building had not existed it is unlikely that the 'Indian' style would have been used here. It is a mad jumble of Islamic and Indian architectural motifs, unrelated to time or culture, but made into a great folly of a room. Imagine a room embracing Romanesque, Perpendicular, Palladian and Gothic elements and one has an idea of the confusion of styles. The Indian Hall is a welcoming room, full of light and interest, in strong contrast to the Singh wing which has not been lived in since the war. Furniture seems superfluous, for nothing can match the proportions or the profusion of styles hewn out of marble by Italian craftsmen (to add a final bizarre touch). The dome above is lit at night by a galaxy of electric bulbs hidden in the cornice at the base. Pity the electrician up there on his padded ladder! If Sir Caspar Prudon Clarke had been active in the era of the super cinema he might have become really famous; he assisted the architects William and Clyde Young (father and son) in their work here with his knowledge of Islamic and Indian stylistic details. When Augustus Hare visited on 14 November 1895 he noted: 'floated here in the luxurious saloon carriage of a private train ... much of his [Duleep Singh's] decoration remains and the delicate white stucco work has a pretty effect when mingled with groups of tall palms and flowering plants. Otherwise the house is almost appallingly luxurious, such masses of orchids, electric light every-where etc. However a set-off the other way is an electric piano which goes on pounding away by itself with a pertinacity which is painfully distracting. In the evenings singing men and dancing women are brought down from London and are supposed to entertain the Royal guest [the Duke of York, later King George V].'

No amount of heat could warm this great room and how cold it was to dance in can be imagined. The floor is said to be sprung with railway buffers (although there is no record of dancing elephants). In the 'new' wing are glorious Edwardian rooms of Ritz style and decoration. We also find the second Lady Iveagh turning a gloomy cavern of a north-facing room into a glamorous bedroom, completed for her in around 1930 by Betty Joel; with black carpet and silvered walls and door it contained a giant's version of her Savoy Hotel furniture in dark hardwoods lined with camphor. This is a house to remember.

Elveden Hall

The Indian Hall

Sledmere House
The Humberside House of
Sir Tatton Sykes Bart

AROUND this house stretches a park by Capability Brown and within is one of the grandest neo-Roman rooms in England. The long Library (page 92) fully rivals that of Adam at Luton Hoo and was initially remarkable for the barrel-vaulted decorated ceiling running one hundred and fifty feet across the house, the carpets echoing the design above. All in the best Adam tradition, but the surprise lay in the fact that it was all conceived by Joseph Rose Jr, working independently of Adam and exhibiting capabilities all of his own. This was in 1794, when the third generation of the Sykes family to live at Sledmere received a baronetcy. Successive generations have also loved the house; so that when it was badly damaged by fire in 1911 it was soon the subject of a superb restoration programme under the supervision of Sir Mark Sykes, sixth Baronet. The present Library is a reconstruction of the original by the local firm of Brierley – as the fashionable firms of Lenygon and Morant, White Allom and Trollopes were all at work re-creating such interiors it is interesting to find a local firm being given the chance to perform a fairly sophisticated project. They did not overprettify or elaborate, in fact the substitution of a parquet floor in the Library exactly repeating the pattern of the burnt carpets is a practical idea giving the room an even more neo-Classical look – even if it looks more Russian than English.

Compared to this, the principal guest Bedroom (page 93), is comfortable and luxurious, two factors high on an Edwardian's list of priorities. Warm rugs, the armchair, the sofa with its French lines and the paintings by Luca Giordano and Abraham Breughel all combine to give us this impression. The bed is a pretty version of late-eighteenth-century taste, with extravagant chintz swags and inserts enlivening the monochrome drapery; and in the corner an Empire cheval-glass reflects a superb, gilt Adam overmantel.

English interest in the Middle East is also reflected in this house, an interest that had existed on both a religious and commercial level for many centuries before Byron added romance to a vision of the Orient. In the late nineteenth century enthusiasm was expressed in the use of Moorish motifs in, for example, the tiled room at Leighton House, London, rooms for William Burges round the corner in Melbury Road, even at Cardiff Castle for the Marquess of Bute. The Smoking Room at Sledmere (opposite) was added for Sir Mark Sykes, who was a distinguished soldier and diplomat with a direct interest in the Middle East – he helped draw up the Sykes–Picot Palestine Agreement of 1916. T. E. Lawrence made this typically incisive comment about the Smoking Room's creator: 'the imaginative advocate of unconvincing world movements, Mark Sykes: also a bundle of prejudices, intuitions, half-sciences. . . . He saw the odd in everything and missed the even' (*Seven Pillars of Wisdom*, 1935).

The room was originally planned as a Turkish Bathroom, but the First World War prevented the export of a large number of the specially commissioned tiles from Turkey and the bath was not completed. Apart from the early-nineteenth-century chairs in one corner, the main decoration is Islamic in concept, based on the Sultan's rooms in the Valedih Mosque in Istanbul and re-created by the designer of this room, David Ohanessian, with considerable skill. The light-fitting is a particularly fine piece of decoration, in its own way as good as anything at the Brighton Pavilion. In the corner broods a bronze bust of Sir Mark himself, by Bryant Baker; it is an incongruous touch in the midst of this hectic Orientalism. This was by no means the last 'Moorish' room to be constructed in England. In the late 1920s White Allom created a mosaic-filled Moorish court for Sir Julien Cahn in Leicestershire. Like so much decoration appealing to the English, oriental motifs suggest a warmth and light quite alien to a damp northern climate.

Sledmere House

Opposite The Library *Above* Bedroom

The House of Mrs Pandora Astor
The Boltons, London

Nostalgic decoration is an inherent characteristic of many English houses that extends far beyond any reinterpretation of historic styles. Certain forms reappear in decoration, but are usually given an up-to-date twist that brings them out of the category of purely 'period' decoration – Syrie Maugham's interiors are an example. Here Mrs Pandora Astor set out rather to recapture an 'atmosphere', a loose evocation of past centuries.

There is more than a whiff of decay in this recent exercise in creating an opulent interior of a dead epoch. It is too casual to be a 'goût Rothschild' and too informal to be stagy, although Mrs Astor has acknowledged the influence of Visconti's last film *The Innocents*. Fabrics billow round the huge early Victorian town-house windows and envelop a table like a vast birthday-cake, in a manner that a late-nineteenth-century German handbook on lavish entertaining 'At Home' would have recommended. Chairs are shrouded less with old-fashioned case-covers such as at Calke Abbey (page 60), but more with covers like dust sheets that give the semblance of a Russian country house sighing through the heat of an interminable summer. This is a setting in which things are about to happen. The air of expectancy will be fulfilled by parties of people basking in the welcome of a house designed to entertain. Up the walls spin plates thrown by an invisible juggler, continental chandeliers flash with light, throwing lustre on to the French curves of the fireplace, the gilt and the brocade. Yet it is all part of a masque. The bare stripped boards are those of a set. No fine parquet, no soft Wilton. This is unashamed fantasy garnished with nostalgia.

The Estonian Legation
167 Queen's Gate, Kensington, London

THIS large town house by Sir Mervyn Macartney was completed in 1890 and is the culmination of many influences in English architecture and decoration. Apart from new furnishings, it has remained virtually unchanged since it was finished and so gives us a complete picture of late-Victorian progressive architecture. Macartney was a pupil of Norman Shaw and a keen student of English architecture, cycling all over Britain with his sketchbook: he was an enthusiastic practitioner of revivalist new styles – such as the 'Wrenaissance'. Every detail of the house at Queen's Gate is a reference to some existing building in England, but it would take an eagle eye and keen intelligence to attribute each one. The house externally reflects forms used in English Renaissance architecture. The original owner, Mr Davidson, was a successful sugar merchant and a Governor of the Bank of Mauritius. Macartney obviously saw his client as a modern version of a Renaissance merchant prince, and inside the house his constant references to the English Renaissance style and to Adam assert this in their associations with new money and status.

Two neo-Classical columns, great chunks of alabaster, inspired the central theme of the architectural and interior design which Macartney plotted throughout the building. That theme begins with the Portland stone columns of the portico, is carried through the marble-floored Entrance Hall to the pillared screen dividing Hall and stairwell, and is then continued up through the stairwell and balustrades to the very top of the five-storied house. The large L-shaped Drawing Room is divided by the transluscent columns of alabaster, a form of screen with surrounding cladding and pilasters of the same material. This is a clear reference to the work of Adam (an Adam fanlight is also inserted in the top of the French windows to the right of the fireplace). A fine panelled dado runs all round the room, uniting the high marble chimney-pieces with the mullioned and leaded windows and the elaborately pedimented doorcases. Throughout the house decorations by William Morris, lavish plasterwork, possibly by Hasley Ricardo, light-fittings by Benson and tiles by William de Morgan, all give away the true period of the house and indicate the taste and interests of both owner and architect.

Sir Mervyn was Surveyor of St Paul's Cathedral on his death, by which time the house had ceased to belong to Davidson's widow and had become the residence and offices of the Estonian Legation and Consul General. It was last decorated in 1935 by Hamptons, a large and worthy, if unexciting, firm of decorators. The 1930s Bohemian cut-glass chandeliers glitter above a mixture of French, Baltic and Russian furniture, whilst Mrs Davidson's original Collard and Collard grand piano encased in rosewood stands in the same position it has occupied for almost a century. Hamptons' 'diplomatic' Drawing Room of the 1930s is essentially English in its timelessness, and was designed to be in keeping with the architecture and decoration of the rest of the house. Many of the servants' bells in the basement still have the names of the members of the Davidson family above them, and the old speaking tube running through four stories is in working order. One hundred and sixty-seven Queen's Gate has survived intact the post-war political disputes that have left occupied the country the Legation represents.

The London House of Bernard Nevill Esq.

WHEN Sir Cecil Beaton enthused over the Edwardian era he managed to create a surprisingly frothy parody of the real thing in his drawings of the sets and costumes for *My Fair Lady*. He undoubtedly captured something of the English nostalgia for a 'golden age', just as these rooms do. The Bedroom (pages 100–1) is a confection of over-indulgence that can only arouse our open-mouthed admiration. Elsewhere glass vases, pictures and objects all jostle gently up to the wall surrounding the fireplace in a manner that would even have seemed excessive to our grandparents.

'She did not know that she was walking into a perfect specimen of an Edwardian drawing-room, which at once reflected and embraced, like a mirror and a crystal in one, the happy thoughtlessness of an era gone forever. Yet so it was. No period is so lost as the Edwardian. The state of society that made it possible is more dead than the pre-historic ferns pressed into streaks of coal; that exquisite silliness summed up in the word "Dolly" can never return.' When Stella Gibbons wrote this in her novel *Bassett* in 1934 the Edwardian era was little more than twenty years dead, and many houses remained unchanged in their decoration. Rooms such as these would have been quite familiar if slightly emptier of objects. Certainly the tiled Kitchen (above) with sensible furniture would have been familiar for longer, and is in a style still to be found in many houses, re-created in preference to plastic and steel. Copper pans and a knife-cleaning machine add to the Edwardian illusion.

In the Bedroom we find the fragility of lace evoking a unique sense of luxury. Apart from the money needed to create or maintain such a room in London in the smoggy years of the Edwardian era, such intricacy of design ceased to be fashionable except for evening dresses. As at Nymans (page 24), the dressing-table is given a fragile trousseau of lace and ribbon trimmings, a form of altar to the owner's beauty. The sprigged paper, curvaceous picture frame and furniture of a more conventional English bedroom are in stark contrast to the unabashed hedonism of the bed-covering, as full blown as the roses on the table.

The London House of Bernard Nevill Esq.

The Bedroom

The Chelsea House of
Felix Hope-Nicholson Esq.

THESE ROOMS evoke the England of the cultured upper-middle classes at the height of Britain's Imperial power during the decades before the First World War. Henry James's characters would have felt at home in rooms like these – one can imagine them setting out from here on an expedition to an antique shop, as in *The Golden Bowl* (1904). Or in the paintings of James Tissot this might be the muted, unostentatious background, showing an essentially English restraint that was vanishing by the 1930s.

In the Studio (opposite) is an eclectic array of furniture and objects, unified by a mellow background of dark floorboards, panelled dado and doors. The warm olive green of the ceiling is relieved by a touch of gilt and a terracotta stripe. Even the heavy chandeliers fail to obtrude. When the furniture was bought it was undoubtedly inexpensive and acquired for the interest or beauty of each object. When William Morris wrote 'have nothing in your house, which is not beautiful', the reverberations extended to anyone with aesthetic sensibilities, and rooms like these might have been found in any number of houses from about 1870 to the 1930s. A Dutch marquetry bureau glows beneath a painting of the Orientalist school. The early-eighteenth-century gate-leg table in the centre is surrounded by ladder-back chairs of country origin. Flowers were very much a part of the decorative ideas of the 1880s, and chrysanthemums and asters like those William de Morgan used in tile decoration add a dash of colour on the table.

In the Dining Room (above) the English late-eighteenth-century mahogany table is conveniently made to collapse so that the ends can be used as elliptically-shaped side tables. A set of Regency chairs with an unusual form of sabre leg in the front is placed around the room, which is liberally hung with prints and oil-paintings. The small convex mirror over the door is a version of larger types popular in Regency and William IV dining rooms. They reflect the whole room in miniature and are often said to have been used by butlers and servants who, while busy with dishes on the side table, could survey the main table and so calculate the needs of the diners.

Shaw's Corner
The Hertfordshire House of Mr and Mrs George Bernard Shaw

IT IS SAID that the Shaws bought the house, originally the New Rectory, because they had seen a gravestone in the village churchyard bearing the following inscription:

BORN MARCH 5 1825
DIED FEBRUARY 13 1895
Her time was Short.

Cecil Roberts narrates that soon after his arrival, G.B.S. announced in the village pub: 'I've decided to take a house in the village for my mistress,' and Charlotte Shaw wondered why no-one called on them for over a year. Whatever the truth of these stories, Shaw did live from 1906 to 1950 in this unpretentious red brick house vaguely following the Arts and Crafts style at its most simple, and all the rooms on the ground floor look almost exactly the same as during his lifetime. Quite what one should expect Shaw's home to look like is debatable, but this house is not dissimilar from that of many University dons of the same vintage. It has an academic look with a peculiarly English restraint that suggests a self-depriving celery-and-sandals existence of the utmost hedonism. In the Drawing Room (above) this is partly due to the absence of any curtains to soften the uncompromising off-white and white decoration – Mrs Shaw was no Syrie Maugham. In fact there are some pleasant pieces of furniture scattered around the room, if one can ignore the grotesque and shabby armchairs that nuzzle up to the fire like decrepit bulldogs. The other chairs are late-eighteenth century and like the secretaire and bureau are perfectly respectable antiques, no doubt acquired because they were relatively inexpensive as well as pretty. The busts on the bureau are both by Rodin, the larger of Shaw and the smaller of Balzac; Rodin himself by Prince Paul Troubetskoy sits on a gate-leg table on the left side of the deep bay window. The room is extremely light with fine woodland views, but it is not welcoming and looks uncomfortable:

now a museum, it lacks the human touch that transforms a furnished house into an inviting home.

The Dining Room (above) has more well-made and nicely proportioned English antique furniture, but is dominated by the fireplace, a masterpiece of ill-conceived Arts and Crafts design on which we can see some of the more unexpected manifestations of Shaw's socialist musings and lion-chasing. Ibsen, on the far right, was returned from the framers the day before Shaw died in this very room. To think of the flamboyant G.B.S. entertaining here is to stretch the imagination, although T. E. Lawrence would have been at ease on his visits. Some of the furniture may have come from Shaw's London house, but the curious clash of surroundings and objects, together with a complete disregard for proportion and colour, is a notable achievement which must be partly explained by the presence of Lenin in pride of place amongst the photographs on the mantelpiece. Such a disregard for surroundings is not uncom-mon amongst academics; but this was the home of a witty playwright. He was termed a man of the world, meeting and conversing with the greatest men of his day. Perhaps a lack of visual sense, and the minimal thought apparently given to the decoration of the rooms, is not surprising from one who could write to *The Times* on 28 August 1937 about 'the joyful news that Hitler is now under the thumb of Stalin whose interest in peace is overwhelming. And everyone except myself', he went on, 'is frightened out of his or her wits. Why? Am I mad? If not, why? Why? Why?' He was to be answered a couple of days later by another correspondent, who asked: 'Who is frightened out of his wits? Who? Who? Who?' (Robert Kee, *1939*, 1984).

What a curious figure Shaw was, lumbering around this frigid house in his old tweeds, choosing to work in a revolving summer house in the garden connected with the world by a telephone – adjusted for out-going calls only.

Clouds Hill
The Dorset Retreat of Lawrence of Arabia

Set amongst the wooded slopes of the West Country in the neighbourhood of Wool, this simple building looks no more than the quiet cottage of a farm-worker of the 1900s when seen from the outside. Thomas Hardy was living locally when T. E. Lawrence found the place and rented it in 1923. He had some family connections with the area, members of his father's family lived nearby, but the intention was to make a retreat for himself, as an eventual place of retirement. At the time, Lawrence was in the ranks of the Royal Tank Corps, having failed to find any worthwhile work or satisfactory use for his talents after his dramatic career in the First World War. As both house and interior were gradually repaired and decorated to Lawrence's taste, the present arrangement emerged. Since 1935 little has changed, apart from the removal of some 1,250 books that formed his library. The absence of books gives an excessively spartan air to an already stark interior, and serves to highlight Lawrence's own frugal habits. He demanded little in the way of material possessions and everything in the interior is simple, well made and utilitarian.

The decoration of the house is dictated not simply by Lawrence's near poverty nor just a desire for simplicity but also by his love of great quantities of exposed woodwork. In the main Living Room (opposite and page 108) we seem to be in a comfortable attic with beams and rafters supporting a plank roof. A note of warmth and colour comes from the fireplace of red brick, but this looks slightly sinister as the arrangement of candlesticks suggests an altar. In this room is his gramophone, his only luxurious possession. Having sold his gold dagger he could afford some records and this gramophone, with its fibre needles, sophisticated soundbox and dusting graphite. The horn now strikes an out-dated note. The room has a 'cultish' feeling to it. Light filters in from a skylight and a low window with seats and wooden shutters to either side. It is hard to imagine the great 'T.E.' entertaining soldier friends here on stuffed olives, salted almonds and baked beans with his own blend of china tea. But then it is equally odd to imagine the chocolates

Clouds Hill

Opposite The Living Room *Above* The Study Room

from Gunters', the peach-fed ham or *pâté de foie gras* sent to him at Christmas by Mrs George Bernard Shaw. She also gave Lawrence a huge quantity of good recordings of classical music, as Lawrence earned only three shillings a day in the ranks.

If the feeling of an English cottage is sought it is soon dispelled by the extraordinary Bedroom (page 107), one of such eccentricity that even a monk might shiver. The high bunk-bed is the top of a sensible built-in chest of drawers. Lawrence was of course a small man (5ft 5in.) and his neat figure must be imagined in this peculiar foil-lined room: the foil kept it cool in summer and warm in winter, theoretically. The glass covers reflect another eccentric habit, eating cheese in his Bedroom. His eccentric lifestyle also meant that the house only gained a chemical lavatory for visits by his mother – Lawrence preferred to use the bushes.

The Study Room (above) lined with shelves and photographs is more practical and welcoming. There is undoubtedly a fetishistic quality to the leather 'reading-couch' and the fine cubist armchair, resembling a flying jacket with fine square-shaped and fleece cushions, but this is a practical room designed for cosy evenings.

At Oxford 'T.E.' had been something of a Pre-Raphaelite aesthete, and the more robust writings of William Morris with its socialist musings appealed to him. On his death on 19 May 1935 Lawrence's collection of books still included sixteen by Morris, and in his later years he even evinced some enthusiasm for Lenin. A particular favourite among Morris's work (according to Vyvyan Richards) was *The Roots of the Mountains* (Collected Works), a story of Nordic-Arcadian life in which communities live in 'halls' and everyone is fighting the Huns. Clouds Hill must owe its cultish, Nordic atmosphere to this, and Lawrence's interest in Morris must also explain his purchase of fourteenth-century house timbers for possible future use and his winter trek in the snow to a 'Morris house' at Chipping Camden, where he enthused over 'the large living room with the old open chapel roof'. These youthful experiences undoubtedly explain the decoration of Clouds Hill.

The Former London House of Margaret, Duchess of Argyll
Upper Grosvenor Street, Mayfair

THIS Georgian terraced house was one of the first to be constructed on the Grosvenor Estate. The rooms shown here were all decorated by Mrs Syrie Maugham for the mother of the Duchess of Argyll, Mrs George Whigham, in 1936. Her scheme is superimposed on earlier decoration for a previous inhabitant by the royal decorators, White Allom, masters of 'Millionaires Georgian'. Syrie Maugham decorated both this house and the Duchess's first house in Regent's Park at the same time. Upper Grosvenor Street is really more the Duchess's house than her mother's, for it was closed during most of the war and the Duchess lived in it for the next thirty-five years or so. It is impossible to look at these rooms and not see her elegant figure there, for these are rooms created as a background for sophisticated living.

It is in a suggestion of warmth and light that is alien to Britain and more suggestive of southern climates that Mrs Maugham's triumph as a decorator is to be found. Apart from the Venetian mirrors and cut-glass chandeliers of the Drawing Room, the theme was fully evident in the Bedroom (opposite and above), which, with the Bathroom (pages 112–13) and connecting Dressing Room, occupied the whole of the second floor. The Bedroom's rich effect of simple light colours, from cream to white, dusty pink to pale blue, was not merely a subtle background for the inhabitants; it blatantly proclaimed expensive luxury in the middle of a grimy city. The interiors did not reflect their London surroundings although they were fully in the English tradition of decoration.

The bed was of film-set proportions, the design in the neo-Greek style of Robsjohn-Gibbings. The draperies round the *chinoiserie* decoration softened the hard, painted surfaces of the walls. Decorative pilasters were inlaid with sparkling panels of mirror and gave unexpected dimensions. On the Maugham tables were her glass lamps: most of the furniture was originally supplied from her shop. The built-in cupboards (probably by White Allom) held shoes. The chimney-piece was the focal point, undiminished by the well-draped bay window flanked by late Regency furniture. All the

The Former London House of Margaret, Duchess of Argyll

Above and opposite The Bathroom

fabrics were faithfully replaced as they became worn.

Just as the silks and satins were part of Mrs Maugham's epoch, so innovative bathroom design was a feature of decoration at the time. For Mrs Whigham she constructed a fantastic room with various parts mirrored, giving a unique and magical look. The fittings were the most modern American ones of the period, showing how remarkably up to date Mrs Maugham was. Yet she never lost track of the style of the house and on one side of the room there is a 1930s chromed fireplace with a pair of upholstered chairs and a stool between them: what arrangement could be more English?

Some of the work in this house echoes that of her friend, the pioneering Elsie de Wolfe, Lady Mendl, but Mrs Maugham showed more ingenuity in handling some unpromising rooms with style. The Duchess recalls her formidable methods: objects would be rejected, but return again and again. She says that her mother preferred and chose Mrs Maugham because their tastes were similar. Neither had a reverence for strict application of stylistic periods and details. Both liked an elegant mixture of comfortable objects and furniture. Syrie Maugham, Mrs Whigham and the Duchess 'hated mahogany'. Mr Whigham was not too keen on Mrs Maugham; he chose the sober pine-panelled library.

In 1941 Peter Quennell captioned a Cecil Beaton photograph of Syrie Maugham's work thus: 'with off-white upholstery went pickled oak side tables and baroque accessories denuded of the paintwork they demanded and deserved. Such an interior was smart, chilly, entirely impractical, and for many reasons, including the gullibility of the rich and the ingenuity of fashionable interior decorators, extraordinarily expensive.' How wrong Mr Quennell was. This house was loved for over four decades and maintained with great care. It was welcoming and had a shimmering quality encapsulated in the Bathroom. This room was turned down by the Victoria and Albert Museum, London, when the Duchess left the house in 1978. We can see here Mrs Maugham's genius in going towards an excess that is firmly held in check.

The Brighton Flat
of the Late Martin Battersby

THIS ROOM in Brighton was intended to display an interesting collection of items from the 1920s and 1930s. Martin Battersby was most famous as a *trompe-l'oeil* artist, although he had also been active as a set-designer for the stage. His diverse work is to be found in private New York elevators, in fine apartments and in the houses of the rich or famous (such as Lady Diana Cooper, page 120). In his own tiny flat Battersby created a glittering jewel-box that shows his great enthusiasm for the styles of the 1920s. By lining the walls with a cunning paper of silvery-gold, Klimt-like design he suggests the ground colouring of a Japanese screen, and therefore by implication echoes the work of the French genius in lacquer, Jean Dunand. One vase by Dunand can be seen in each window; they date from the mid-1920s, and Dunand also worked on the rare bronze-framed lacquer cabinet by Eugen Printz that stands between the windows. Above a Neilz vase hangs a Bakst ballet design evoking the heyday of the Ballets Russes in the 1920s. French

chairs of earlier in that decade show the curious blending of French Louis XVI forms with German and Austrian pre-First World War decorative details. The rather hard appearance of the *moiré* and silk furnishing fabrics suggests a brittle 'chic' and contrasts with the exuberant display cabinet. To one side is a marble-topped wrought-iron side table not unlike those by Edgar Brandt.

A Chinese coromandel lacquer screen is an echo of the 'Chinese craze' of the 1920s for lacquerwork and *chinoiserie* decoration; it becomes an amusing backdrop for a good Ruhlmann table of burr amboyna and ivory holding a collection of miscellaneous objects – including cigarette cases of Paul Brandt and Fabergé with a typical and slightly kitsch lamp by the Parisian Roland.

With such a plethora of valuable objects displayed in this manner there is an air of being in a rather good shop, particularly as the floor is devoid of the coverings necessary to give a softer look to the often severe outlines.

The Homewood
The Surrey House of Patrick Gwynne Esq.

WHEN Margot Beste-Chetwynde asked Professor Silenius for a new house in Evelyn Waugh's *Decline and Fall* (1928), it was 'something clean and square' that she had in mind. She should have been given this house. Designed in 1937 by the present owner Mr Patrick Gwynne, then in partnership with Wells Coates, it was built for the former's parents and is one of the few twentieth-century domestic buildings to be protected by a Preservation Order. For sheer excellence of congenial design and construction it is probably unrivalled. The sprung maple floor of the Living Room (opposite) has a golden warmth of its own and was designed for dancing; 'Cocktails and laughter. But what comes after? Nobody knows,' wrote Noel Coward. The natural successor, High Tech, seems a vulgar sham compared to the materials used here.

White leather is used to pad the doors to the Living Room, which are surrounded by an aluminium frame set in a wall of grey-tinted mirror (above). An elegantly curved staircase is constructed of the artificial stone mixture known as 'Terrazzo' with an ebonized liner-style hand-rail. The well is lit from below by a ground-glass panel in the floor, casting light up to the antique Bristol-glass chandelier. This was found by Mr Gwynne's father and incorporated as a daring Le Corbusier touch reminiscent of the effects achieved in the apartment of Carlos de Béstigui in Paris.

The Living Room is divided by a black-grey wall of Levanto marble in which a fire blazes. This wall is continued with a folding screen, and beyond is the Dining Room and a terrace with staircases to both roof and garden. Much of the furniture was designed by Mr Gwynne, including the glass-topped table; the reclining chairs are early examples by Bruno Matthsson. The right-hand wall is veneered in rosewood and contains tambour-fronted cupboards.

This large area is all on the first-floor level, apart from the kitchen all the service areas are below. The views over the grounds from the Living Room are therefore unimpeded and show the gardens off. The panorama changes with the seasons and is part of the decoration of the room, like a large Japanese screen.

The Belgravia House of
Mr and Mrs Hugh Clifford-Wing

WHEN Mr and Mrs Clifford-Wing moved into this Georgian town house in 1955 they found a light sunny house with a good parquet floor in the first-floor Drawing Room, good proportions, and little else. As the owner is a professional decorator who began his career with the old-established London firm of Trollopes in the 1930s, he has been able to exploit the potential of the house to full advantage. Experience of the great years of decorating for a variety of clients, including palaces and yachts, was brought to bear on a conventional interior and every last detail has been used to effect. The owner's wife has converted a room at the turn of the stairs between ground and first floor into a charming garden room with a small terrace beyond; and the basement now includes an Office and Studio, as well as retaining the Kitchen.

In the master Bedroom light colours are an unashamed reflection of fashionable taste in the 1930s and 1940s. The soft pinkish background is muralled with pale blue and grey scenes by Peter Stebbing, who has done similar work in Greek villas for several of Mr Clifford-Wing's clients. This decoration is in a style reminiscent of 'Chinese' painting exported to England in the eighteenth century, and is also seen in the Bathroom next door. Here solid old fittings are the chief ingredients in the room's success. Chintz curtains, a covered stool, a close-fitted carpet: all proclaim the room to be as English as the charmingly antiquated taps and lavatory cistern with domed porcelain lid. Warm towels stand ready at the foot of the splendidly deep old-fashioned bath, near the no-nonsense set of scales in the window. The charm of such a room depends on its mixture of functional and luxurious touches: so the substantial eighteenth-century tall-boy on the other side of the room contrasts with the generous chintz curtains and electric wall-heater. It all creates the feeling of a comfortable and practical bathroom, on a less imposing scale but in the same spirit of fun as that of Syrie Maugham in the Duchess of Argyll's house (page 113).

A Knightsbridge Town House

A STONE'S THROW from Harrods, this house has all the brittle chic of a sophisticated London house, but differs from Mr Clifford-Wing's house of similar size and layout (opposite) by its use of striking pieces of furniture. The owner spent some time as an assistant to John Fowler, who gave advice on the decoration of this terraced house. Its clean lines and light colours reflect the less hectic decorative styles of the 1950s and early 1960s, before the invasion of bright colours, patterns, glass and chrome.

One end of the cool off-white and grey first-floor Drawing Room is dominated by a glistening 1930s grand piano of unusual design, and the other is filled with comfortable seating arrangements. A considerable amount of the room's charm lies in its airy quality, epitomized by the painted and decorated chairs – some are eighteenth century. A solid and architectural bookcase is built up against one wall (facing the fireplace) and is painted in sympathy with walls and woodwork; a clock, two covered, urn-shaped vases known as cassolettes, and plates are ranged along the shelf. An orange tree stands on a 'cloud-table'. This table forms an unusual link between the elements of eighteenth-century decoration in the room and the last introduction of an unusual style in the 1940s. It was a style evolved in Scandinavia in the late 1930s, picked up by French designers after the Second World War and brought to prominence in England after the festival of Britain in 1951. It was around that time that this table was purchased by the owner, then an Oxford undergraduate, an original having been used by Jean Royère in a scheme in Paris in 1946. As with the emergence of *art déco* as a collector's style, the products of the 1950s are now enjoying a new vogue; few examples, however, are of as high quality as this cloud-table. Other notable features of the room are the simple French furniture and needlepoint rugs, both elements of John Fowler's style in the 1950s and also seen in Mrs Lancaster's flat in Avery Row (pages 124–7). Elaborately draped curtains give a final touch of colour and grandeur to a sophisticated scheme that is a triumph of subtle understatement.

The London House of Lady Diana Cooper, Little Venice

LADY DIANA COOPER's three volumes of autobiography have decorative end-papers reproducing *trompe-l'oeil* panels painted for her by Martin Battersby to hang in her former house in Chantilly. It was there that she and her husband lived after he ceased to be Ambassador to France, and the panels are painted with mementoes and vignettes of her life. They now hang at the dining end of the L-shaped Drawing Room (these pages) in her London house, a quiet building in the solid neo-Classical manner of the early decades of the nineteenth century.

In the 1930s Lady Diana was one of the few enthusiasts of both the Regency and Empire styles. Her previous London house reflected this taste, but her residence at the British Embassy in Paris no doubt gave her a surfeit of the style. This house accommodates the mementoes of a long and eventful life.

With English ingenuity the downstairs Cloakroom (page 123) is given a highly personal mixture of decorative elements. Amongst the solid fittings is a galaxy of pictures and photographs, many depicting members of the Royal Family. No need to dig out albums or clutter the place with frames, for the photographs can be viewed and scrutinized at leisure. A potentially dull room is given immediate interest and a very individual style.

The Hall (page 122) of her present house is left to rely on its fine architectural proportions and stone-flagged floor, while the Drawing Room has achieved the English style that comes from a judicious mixture of French and English taste, of periods and of decorative styles. In the Hall a welcoming array of glasses forms a self-service alternative to a butler's pantry, and above is a portrait of Lady Diana by Ambrose McEvoy. In the Drawing Room comfortable sofas and armchairs are devoid of strict formality, screens break the firm lines of the proportions of the room and painted chairs give light and movement. For the room has a vivacity that reflects the owner, while the colours echo the gardens outside. It has a countrified look that marks it as English, an effect that stems from Lady Diana's instinctive handling of the decoration.

The London House of Lady Diana Cooper

Above The Hall *Opposite* The Cloakroom

The Former London House
of Mrs Nancy Lancaster, Avery Row, Mayfair

DITCHLEY PARK by Gibbs and Kent (page 35), Kelmarsh and Haseley Court are all fine eighteenth-century houses once lived in by the Virginian-born Mrs Lancaster, owner of Colefax & Fowler from 1944 to 1960. These rooms 'above the shop' were hers until 1980, and now form part of the premises of Colefax & Fowler itself. The yellow Drawing Room (opposite) is now empty of her furniture and reveals the colours she used to create its sumptuous effect, a decorative technique she also used in the decoration of her country houses.

This Drawing and Dining Room was once part of Sir Jeffry Wyatville's offices, leased to him in 1821. It was probably used by his draughtsmen and is 16 feet wide and 46 feet long with three large and deep windows overlooking a small garden to the side of the old Bath Club. Completely hidden from the street, Mrs Lancaster turned the room into a perpetually sunny living room and achieved an English look of countrified sophistication in the city. This look was also a speciality of her partner and collaborator John Fowler: his decoration of another unusual building nearby for the elegant Mrs Jack Dennis achieved a similar effect of light and space. Both appeared to be large houses at a time when the 'London house' was shrinking in size.

A description of the room a few years after its completion sums up what was then considered a great achievement: 'Yellow rather than cream! Thus the walls are a semi-gloss Pekin yellow, the ceiling is painted in three tones of subtle beige; the cornice and high skirting-board are *trompe-l'oeil* simulating sienna marble. The curtains are in two shades of golden yellow taffeta and shantung and hang from gilded wooden rods with brown and yellow cords. Sofas and armchairs are covered in deep citrus yellow shantung with heavy fringes to match. And, marigold yellow cushions. The gilt chairs are covered in a special chintz copied from an 1840 design. The yellow background of the magnificent Ukrainian rug before the fireplace sets the theme' (*House and Garden Book of Interiors*, 1962). The use of colour shows an ingenuity typical of John Fowler, an expert in this field. The assembly of various objects achieves a rare harmony, a look of having grown slowly rather than just being acquired. This is very English. Pieces of mirror around the doors, the bookcases, lamps, gilt wall-lights and a blackamoor stool are all inventive touches achieving a balance and symmetry, in keeping with the scale of the room.

The Former London House of Mrs Nancy Lancaster

Above The Bathroom *Opposite* The Bedroom

The quiet little Bedroom (opposite) is a complete contrast, with cool off-white and bluish-grey giving a slightly French flavour to the overall effect. A surprisingly jazzy lacquered early-eighteenth-century bureau-bookcase lends a sparkle to the room, and the simple Bathroom beyond (above) contains old engravings depicting bulbs. Mrs Lancaster has said that she likes a mixture of styles and objects appropriate to a room, together with a sense of scale: 'As in a salad the ingredients should "marry well" – although I am probably better at rooms than salads.'

The Dower House, Badminton
The Former House of the Duke and Duchess of Beaufort

DOMINATED by a beautiful English chimney-piece, this Drawing Room epitomizes the look so often sought by decorators in their attempts to create an 'English' room and so rarely achieved. The sienna and white statuary marble chimney-piece sits in the centre of the room, a carved panel depicting a classical scene – a favourite device of the late eighteenth century. Above it is an array of postcards which reduces the extreme formality of a beautiful portrait to a more domestic scale; this is a room to be lived in rather than just looked at. Amusing needlework bell-pulls give a sense of scale to either side of the chimney-piece. For chilly days a stack of logs stands ready to give a good blaze in the grate, and the club fender has a welcoming look.

The room is also a study and library, so wall space for pictures is restricted. The solution has been overcome by the use of an easel and a stand, and the paintings are given a setting that is dignified and yet does not detract from the subject matter. The chintz upholstery plays a prominent part in the decoration. Although not much is used, the eye is drawn to it, and the flowery pattern is so peculiarly English that it stamps the room with its rosy personality. Chintz-covered sofa and chairs sit on an old carpet, and fringes to both table draperies and covers are echoed in the details on the curtains, in turn suspended from a mahogany pole over the arched French windows. Other furniture in the room includes a useful pedestal desk and low tables made from eighteenth-century mahogany trays on modern stands. Flowers, plants and lamps made from old vases inject fresh colours into this pleasing English room.

The London House
of Stephen Long Esq.

THE ENGLISH are a nation of collectors. At Calke Abbey (pages 60–4) successive generations left accumulations of carefully hoarded clutter. Old ladies die pinioned beneath heaps of preserved copies of the *Daily Beast* that have collapsed into the walkways that remain of their rooms. Recently a fleet of lorries removed the accumulated junk of a lifetime from a modest house in the North of England: everything had been kept, including canned food decades old. Such clutter takes control by its sheer volume. Fortunately, the owner of this room has an eye for colour and juxtaposition of objects that is savagely keen; in spite of the extraordinary number of objects in the room he has maintained perfect control – just.

A warm yellow background creates a glowing effect, heightened by the boldly patterned carpet with its crowns and Tudor roses that hint at a royal provenance. Generously large curtains are echoed in the swags and bows of the ribbons above the portraits, adding to the lush feeling of almost suffocating hospitality. On bookcase and table are a selection of black busts, porcelain and objects of some interest and importance to their owner as 'household gods', irrespective of their value. (The 'Delft' ginger jars are in reality only painted old tobacco pots.) Their arrangement is a work of art, beside which a David Hicks 'tablescape' would be reduced to the level of a Boots countertop. A dozen early-nineteenth-century Davenport botanical dessert plates are ranged above the desk; over the fireplace hangs a triple portrait of Charles I (a contemporary copy of the famous Van Dyck); and below that is a collection of red pottery, some from the Isleworth factory of Shore & Goulding and some from Bohemia; all jostle for space and attention in a manner that most people would find overpowering. It defies any personality but that of the owner – and why not? It is fully in the tradition of creating one's own surroundings in one's own way, much as Mole loved his own little house in Kenneth Grahame's *The Wind in the Willows*. Calke Abbey, the interior of a country cottage, this London house: all are equally an expression of the English spirit of individuality.

Two Interiors Designed by David Hicks Esq.

David Hicks's look is Syrie Maugham in hell. Where she conjured soft curves and pastel shades with a wave of a braceletted wrist, Mr Hicks takes a straight line to vibrant colour. No detail has escaped his scrutiny, from bathrooms to letter-boxes he has pronounced a verdict, with succinct explanation he has reduced everything to bare essentials. From Totnes to Tokyo his name is synonymous with Good Taste. His first books in the 1960s showed him to be a ruthless dictator, so that when the 'tablescapes' at his last country house, Britwell Salome, were sold, the plans for reconstruction in less aesthetic hands went with them. ('Tablescapes' are arrangements of objects on a table, a decorative feature devised and much used by David Hicks.) He has a clear style and a distinctive panache visible in every room and where he treads carpets take on geometric patterns.

In his own red-hued London Bedroom (opposite) are many historical references: covered vases, a bust, canopied bed and severely Louis XVI chimney-piece. The mirror and lighting keep any tendency towards a mere period pastiche firmly in check, but Mr Hicks has himself described his flat as 'an atmosphere in antiquity'. Originally a cornice ran along the top of the 1930s cupboards, but this was removed and the cupboards were re-decorated to produce what Hicks describes as a 'dramatic and unexpected support for the urns' (*Living with Design*, 1979). Symmetry and order are plainly part of the decorative scheme. The aggressive geometric carpet and gilt table are unusual components in a bedroom, and this one is very much Hicks 'decorated' – as is the Drawing Room in his present country house (above).

Shades of pink, mustard, brown and white are the main colours here and the combination could be fatal. But Mr Hicks skates on thin ice with all the confidence we expect of the English tradition and continues to take the prizes for practical backgrounds that form undemanding interiors for life today.

A Country House
Decorated by David Mlinaric Esq.

THESE ROOMS in a country house reflect an approach to interior design and decoration that now seems slightly *démodé*, emerging as it did during the mid-1960s. Muted backgrounds, patches of colouring in textiles, a few pieces of carefully chosen furniture, all these are framed by stripped floorboards. Parallel to this approach was the look inspired by 'Habitat' shops, with simple modern furniture and one carefully positioned 'antique'. Both forms of decoration suffer the disadvantage of being in such good taste that they become bland. Handled by David Mlinaric, a prominent initiator and master of a sophisticated development of these styles, the results achieve subtlety and distinction, as seen here.

The owner is an antique dealer, and Mr Mlinaric has combined some good antique furniture and porcelain to create a look of understated elegance. Both rooms are dominated by pleasantly simple fireplaces and built-in cupboards, which have been painted inside and filled with a colourful array of Chinese export porcelain and metal objects. The cupboards are thus made into a feature, the

doors hanging open to reveal the contents. A loose evocation of the eighteenth century is there, a period explored by Mr Mlinaric in his justly famous restoration work for the National Trust.

The Dining Room (opposite) has light fresh colours and a pretty landscape in the overmantel is part of the comfortable countrified atmosphere. A late-eighteenth-century mahogany breakfast table is surrounded by curvaceous decorated chairs in the style of the early part of that century.

In the Sitting Room (above) an unusual standing oil lamp has been electrified and placed next to an early-nineteenth-century Anglo-Indian chair. The boldly patterned carpet and brass table conjure up the idea of the British Empire and travel abroad, as so often expressed in English country houses.

This is all so typically English that one looks for the discordant note, an ugly souvenir or some grotesque object. They are naturally not there – and this is the difference between a decorator's carefully styled room and one evolved by the owner himself.

Charleston Manor
The Former Sussex House of Vanessa Bell

THERE is something about these rooms which suggests both the best and the worst of English decoration, and it is irresistible as well as slightly repellent. There is certainly a naïve quality, a schoolroom exultation in the joy of vivid effects, bold strokes and lush patterns. But it is a very knowing naïvety. The colours are more subtle than those of the fairground or the decorated barge, the forms and patterns being more delicate than our almost extinct 'folk-art'. It reflects a painter's urge to colour everything in sight.

Charleston Manor is an eighteenth-century farmhouse nestling in beautiful Sussex downland, and was the home of the painters Vanessa Bell and Duncan Grant. Between 1919 and 1939 it was used by them mainly as a 'holiday' house (although in those days that meant all the summer months), but every year Vanessa became more reluctant to leave it and lived there permanently after the Second World War. When she moved to Charleston in 1916 it required an immense amount of work to make it habitable, although such a rambling house could never be made really convenient or even particularly warm – it had no piped water or electricity. Comfort was low on the list of priorities. With the highly developed visual sense of a painter, Mrs Bell gradually added pattern and colour to the low-ceilinged, generously proportioned rooms, using a warm but neutral background of grey distemper to throw the colours out. She devised exuberant geometrical motifs to decorate and link together fireplaces, doors, overmantels, walls and furniture. The rooms were not furnished all at once, instead odd and often unusual pieces of furniture appeared over the years. This is an artist's home: and by the 1940s when Vanessa Bell, Duncan Grant and their daughter Angelica were all painting the smell of paint was everywhere.

Charleston was a meeting place for some of the Bloomsbury set. John Maynard Keynes, Lytton Strachey, David Garnett and Vanessa's sister Virginia Woolf were all frequent visitors – 'Very plain living and high thinking,' was Vita Sackville-West's comment on lunch there. Taken piece by piece the decoration of the rooms has little impact, but it is all done in the confident and individual style that is characteristic of Bloomsbury taste. In Raymond Mortimer and Dorothy Todd's *The New Interior Decoration* of 1929 it is amazing to find Grant's painted decoration of a Cambridge don's rooms featured amongst the austere lines of Le Corbusier and the Bauhaus. Todd summed up the look as something uniquely British in an essay *The Modern Interior* published in the same year: 'a compromise characteristic of the British temperament is being effected which does not break too ruthlessly with the time-hallowed domesticity of London. The Englishman will be allowed to remain in his castle and not be turned violently into his steam-ship or electric yacht.'

There is nothing in Charleston to suggest the twentieth century of Cubism or Expressionism, or even the new forms of design. The peculiar Englishness of such rooms as these is emphasized by Dorothy Todd: '. . . such as Mr Duncan Grant, Mrs Clive Bell, Mr Douglas Davidson, Mr Alan Walton and Mr McKnight Kauffer have produced a style of decoration suitable for the eighteenth-century houses which are still such a delicious feature of British civilization. But they will never think of copying a Louis XV sofa or a Beauvais tapestry. They rather seek to discover and isolate what was ultimately essential in the eighteenth century and re-invigorate that spirit with the oxygen of today.'

At Charleston the results of this approach are quite unique. In front of the Dining Room fireplace (opposite) is an enormous table made bright by the application of a blobby form of decoration. An Italian painted side table gives a dash of exoticism as does the construction of the lampshade, like some antique Roman pot on display. The arrangement of a few objects in the Sitting Room (pages 138–9) is reflected in Vanessa's still-life of them, set against a wall freely decorated with a design resembling a feathery Paisley pattern. Grant's mural above the fireplace is surprisingly moving both in its directness and because of the oddity of finding such a subject in this house. And there is much here that is odd: Grant and Bell even painted the feathers of the white chickens in the yard, as well as the woodwork, furniture and paintings.

The appeal of this Bloomsbury-decoration was short-lived, for the British are quickly bored of intellectual snobbery and there was a great deal involved here: 'On my first afternoon I proudly hung a reproduction of Van Gogh's "Sun-flowers" over the fire and set up a screen, painted by Roger Fry with a Provençal landscape, which I had bought inexpensively when the Omega workshops were sold up. I displayed also a poster by McKnight Kauffer and Rhyme Sheets from the Poetry Bookshop, and, most painful to recall, a porcelain figure of Polly Peachum which stood between black tapers on the chimney-piece . . . but it was not until Sebastian, idly turning the page of Clive Bell's *Art*, read: "Does anyone feel the same kind of emotion for a butterfly or a flower that he feels for a cathedral or a picture?" "Yes, *I* do!" that my eyes were opened' (Evelyn Waugh, *Brideshead Revisited*, 1945).

Charleston Manor

The Sitting Room

Brief Notes on some Designers and Architects mentioned in the Text

ROBERT ADAM (1728–91)   Together with his brother James (1732–94), he created a light neo-Classical style of architecture and interior decoration. Trained by his architect father in Edinburgh, then in Rome where he was in contact with Clérisseau and Piranesi, Adam made an extensive study of Roman decoration and colouring. The result of his researches and training is to be seen in the decoration of Kedleston Hall (pages 38–9), Syon House (pages 40–3) and Nostell Priory (pages 46–9). At Nostell the furniture by Chippendale is a particularly successful example of the Adam style. Adam also designed in the Gothick manner at Alnwick (pages 72–3), but his reputation rests on virtuoso adaptions of Roman styles and motifs for a remarkable variety of buildings and interiors in town and country.

GIOVANNI BAGUTTI (1681–c.1730)   Italian master plasterer whose elaborate work can be seen at Ditchley Park (page 35).

SIR CHARLES BARRY (1795–1860)   Architect of the Palace of Westminster in a revival of the English Perpendicular style. He also practised in the more domestic surroundings of Highclere (pages 58–9) and Toddington and his versatility extended to neo-Renaissance architecture as seen in the Travellers' and Reform Clubs in London.

MARTIN BATTERSBY (1919–82)   *Trompe-l'oeil* painter, decorator, textile and stage designer. He was an early exponent of the *Art nouveau* revival and the author of books on this and on decoration in the 1920s and 1930s.

WILLIAM ARTHUR SMITH BENSON (1854–1928)   Metalworker, architect and designer. A collaborator of William Morris who encouraged his work, Benson produced a range of designs through his own factory for Morris & Co.

LANCELOT 'CAPABILITY' BROWN (1716–83)   Exponent of 'natural' landscaping of parklands and gardens.

WILLIAM BURGES (1827–81)   Architect and designer in a lavish interpretation of a medieval Gothic style. Cardiff Castle is a triumph of his romantic medievalism.

THOMAS CHIPPENDALE (1718–79)   The son of a Yorkshire carpenter, he became a successful businessman in charge of large workshops supplying all the necessities of house furnishing and decoration. His three editions of *The Gentleman and Cabinet Maker's Director* (first edition, 1754) show a wide variety of designs in Gothick, *chinoiserie* and a light Rococo, but some of his finest work was done under Adam's influence at Nostell (pages 46–9), a masterful display of marquetry and carving in the neo-Classical style. His son Thomas (1749–1822) worked with him and, after his death, carried on the family business.

HUGH CLIFFORD-WING (born 1914)   Decorator who began his career with the old-established firm of Trollopes in the early 1930s. His diverse range of styles was undoubtedly a result of the extensive training and experience acquired in such a huge firm and his work has included the royal palaces in Athens and Nepal, yachts, castles, Greek villas and houses in Norway as well as offices and houses in England.

WELLS COATES (1895–1958)   Architect and designer. He was in partnership with Patrick Gwynne from 1935 to 1938 (when 'The Homewood', illustrated on pages 116–17, was completed). An exponent of the most recent designing techniques and of modern design and architecture, Coates was interested in simple mass-housing experiments, but remains most famous for his work at the BBC headquarters at Broadcasting House, and the Lawn Road Flats in Hampstead, London.

COLEFAX & FOWLER   Founded by Lady Colefax in collaboration with the London dealers Stair and Andrew in 1934, joined by John Fowler in 1938, and acquired by Nancy Lancaster in 1950, this London firm of decorators has come to symbolize a uniquely English form of decoration based on the distinctive styles of its influential owners.

JEAN DUNAND (1877–1942)   Swiss-born metal craftsman who worked in France, he made an extensive study of the use of lacquer and enamel. His vases, panels and furniture are particularly prized by collectors of the products of the 1920s and 1930s.

PETER CARL FABERGÉ (1846–1920)   Working in Russia, this master goldsmith and jeweller had extensive workshops supplying luxuriously elegant jewellery, jewelled enamelled objects and carved hardstone pieces to his shop. His Easter eggs for the Czarina were a particularly triumphant blend of metalwork, enamelling and jewellery.

JOHN FOWLER (1906–77)   One of the most influential decorators of the twentieth century, he had an extensive knowledge of English decoration throughout the centuries, and his use of textiles, furniture and colour could achieve spectacular effects in a modern idiom based upon this knowledge. A partner of Sybil Colefax and Nancy Lancaster, Fowler produced a wide variety of work ranging from fresh interpretations of eighteenth-century ideas to completely faithful reconstructions of historic interiors for the National Trust.

PATRICK GWYNNE (born 1913)   In partnership with Wells Coates from 1935 to 1938, he is one of the finest architects and designers to practice in the style of the Modern Movement in England. He has created a relatively small number of buildings since 1938, but all share a remarkably high level of excellence in design and choice of material. Houses for the late Lawrence Harvey in London and California showed his adaptability to surroundings and climate. His restaurant buildings in Hyde Park and the interior of a recently reconstructed flat on Green Park reveal an elegant ingenuity that is rare in modern architecture.

THOMAS HOPE (1796–1831)   Of independent means, Hope was a patron of the arts and an enthusiastic researcher of antique Greek and Egyptian decoration, producing designs for furniture in these styles. He published his influential *Household Furniture and Decoration* in 1807.

BETTY JOEL   Active as a designer and decorator in London during the 1920s, 1930s and 1940s, her vast business included a suburban furniture factory and showrooms at Hyde Park Corner which displayed the latest designs in textiles and furnishings.

WILLIAM KENT (1685–1748)   Architect, designer and decorator. Drawing on Italian styles and influenced by Inigo Jones, he created a unique style that fused all the elements of a lavish Italianate architecture with an English restraint. The resulting triumph of his work can be seen at Houghton (pages 36–7), where the choice of subtle colour and fine woods is set against lush plasterwork and fine carving, with a sprinkling of gilding lending highlights to the massive quality of his work.

MRS NANCY LANCASTER   The American-born former owner of Colefax & Fowler, she has collaborated with Stephen Boudin of Jansen (the Parisian decorators) and John Fowler on the creation of fine interiors in her own houses (including Avery Row, pages 124–7 and Ditchley, page 35). She is generally acclaimed as possessing a unique sense of colour and scale.

BATTY LANGLEY (1695–1751)   Designer and author. His first designs for furniture were in the Palladian manner, but his greatest success was his book *Gothic Architecture improved by rules and proportions in many grand designs of columns, doors, windows*. This was a 1747 reissue of *Ancient Architecture Restored and Improved* (1742) and was the beginning of the revival of the style soon to be known as Gothick.

SIR MERVYN MACARTNEY (1853–1932)   Editor of the *Architectural Journal* and an encylopaedic mine of information on all English architectural styles and details, he was a pupil of Norman Shaw and became part of the generation of architects who created new buildings using a reinterpretation of essentially English vernacular styles. He had many links with members of the Arts and Crafts movement.

KARL BRUNO MATTHSSON (born 1907)   Swedish designer of furniture, especially famous for bentwood designs.

SYRIE MAUGHAM (1879–1953)   Wife of Somerset Maugham, she was generally thought of as the creator of the all-white room. In fact, the range of styles and colours which she mastered show that she had a remarkable eye for colour and balance. Although shapes and styles might be 'antique', furnishings were handled in the most modern way and her upholstery was much admired by John Fowler. She created a look of effortless elegance.

WILLIAM DE MORGAN (1839–1917)   Ceramic designer. An associate of William Morris, he produced plates, vases and especially tiles with patterns derived from a variety of sources – Chinese, Persian, Gothic and Greek pottery.

WILLIAM MORRIS (1834–96)   Dissatisfied with mid-Victorian industrially-produced decorative furnishings and furniture, Morris set out to produce new designs. Wallpapers, textiles and furniture were designed by him, often inspired by the simplicity of sixteenth and early-seventeenth-century designs. His own factory, Morris & Co., produced the goods, but Morris was never happy with industrialization and indulged in impractical socialist musings whilst living well from the profits of his enterprises.

JOHN NASH (1752–1835)   Architect. Trained with Sir Robert Taylor and then became a speculative builder before he was employed by the Prince Regent from 1798. He developed Regent Street from 1811 and the Regent's Park area in a stuccoed neo-Classical style. The Royal Pavilion, Brighton, was rebuilt by him (1815–23), he worked at Royal Lodge, Windsor, and began the reconstruction of Buckingham House (1821) which was still unfinished when George IV died in 1830.

OMEGA WORKSHOPS   Founded by Roger Fry in 1913 with the aim of improving design. Furniture and textiles were designed by such artists as Vanessa Bell and Duncan Grant. The workshops closed in 1920.

AUGUSTUS WELBY NORTHMORE PUGIN (1812–52)   Architect and designer in the neo-Gothic manner, and influential enthusiast for the Gothic revival in England. His work at the Houses of Parliament (1836–37) was preceded by his *Gothic Furniture in the Style of the Fifteenth Century* (1835).

TERENCE ROBSJOHN-GIBBINGS (died 1976)   Worked with Lord Duveen's brother in selling antiques and then became a designer and decorator in the late 1930s, specializing in a modern interpretation of antique Greek interiors and furniture. He also produced designs for elegantly simple modern furniture which could be mass produced.

ANTHONY SALVIN (1799–1881)   Architect and designer. From Gothick to Jacobethan Salvin brought a robust touch to his buildings, often extraordinarily elaborate as at Harlaxton in Lincolnshire, or quietly domestic as at Thoresby Hall in Nottinghamshire. Salvin could also create a more chilling form of architecture as in his 'Normanesque' style at Alnwick (pages 72–3). His interiors are all well proportioned and generally pleasingly inventive.

RICHARD NORMAN SHAW (1831–1912)   Architect. Shaw was one of the most influential architects of the nineteenth century. After attending the Architectural School of the Royal Academy, he trained with G.E. Street, so that his early buildings reflect the style of the Gothic revival. His use of the 'Queen Anne' vernacular marked a new departure in nineteenth-century architecture, and his links with and inspiration of the Arts and Crafts Movement were connected with his study of earlier English styles. His eclectic taste embraced sixteenth-century styles of manorial building and even the neo-Baroque of his last years, as seen in the Piccadilly Hotel, London (1905–8). Just as the 'Wrenaissance' of his earlier years inspired such architects as Sir Mervyn Macartney (167 Queen's Gate), so his neo-Baroque had a profound influence on British building for the next thirty years. He is also credited with the first garden suburb of Bedford Park, London (1877).

SIR JEFFREY WYATVILLE (1760–1840)   Architect of the remodelling of Windsor Castle under George IV (1824–8). He was a nephew of James Wyatt (1747–1813) who was one of the most fashionable architects of his time and a master of the neo-Classical style as well as the romantic Gothick as seen in his designs for Fonthill Abbey. Wyatville added to his name in accordance with early-nineteenth-century pretensions to an ancient lineage and Norman connections, and practised in his architecture a romantic sham medievalism.

Acknowledgements

The authors and publishers would like to express their gratitude to Her Majesty Queen Elizabeth The Queen Mother for graciously permitting the inclusion of the Saloon at Royal Lodge, and to the many other owners of the rooms depicted in this book: Mrs Pandora Astor; Margaret, Duchess of Argyll; The Duke and Duchess of Beaufort; Mona, Countess of Beauchamp; Major Simon Browne; The Earl of Carnarvon; Mr and Mrs Hugh Cavendish; The Marquess of Chomondeley; Mr and Mrs Hugh Clifford-Wing; Lady Diana Cooper; The Ditchley Foundation; The Estonian Legation; R.E.J. Compton Esq. (Newby Hall is open to the public daily from 1 April to 1 October); The Greater London Council (for 18 Stafford Terrace); Patrick Gwynne Esq.; Henry Harpur-Crewe Esq.; David Hicks Esq.; Myles Thoroton Hildyard Esq.; Felix Hope-Nicolson Esq.; The Earl of Iveagh; Mrs Knowles; Mrs Nancy Lancaster; Stephen Long Esq.; The National Trust (for Clouds Hill, Shaw's Corner and Nostell Priory – properties of the National Trust); Bernard Nevill Esq.; Lady Rupert Nevill; The Hon. Nigel Nicolson Esq.; The Duke and Duchess of Northumberland; Sir John Ropner; Anne, Countess of Rosse; Lord St Oswald; The Marquess of Salisbury; Viscount Scarsdale; Sir Sacheverell Sitwell; Sir Tatton Sykes Bart; Sir John Wiggin Bart. Especial thanks are due to *Architectural Digest* for permission to reproduce several photographs included here.

Derry Moore wishes to thank particularly Gervase Jackson-Stops for his advice and the following who also gave valuable assistance: Alec Cobbe Esq., Peter Fleetwood-Hesketh Esq., Sir William Dugdale Bart, Ian Grant, Jane Heyworth, Henry Potts, Gavin Stamp and Mrs West de Wend-Fenton. Michael Pick wishes to thank the members of his family and friends who have provided generous hospitality during the preparation of the book and especially Nigel Logan Esq. in whose Casa Cordillera, Tangier, much of this book was written. He would also like to thank Sarah Bevan for her excellent advice and comments and The Revd Julian Browning for literary sources. Both are honoured by the appreciative Foreword by Anne, Countess of Rosse, a notable champion of the English room in all its varieties. They would like to thank all those who allowed their houses to be viewed for the purposes of this book.

Index